Also from GHF Press

Making the Choice
When Typical School Doesn't Fit Your Atypical Child

Forging Paths
Beyond Traditional Schooling

If This is a Gift, Can I Send it Back?
Surviving in the Land of the Gifted and Twice Exceptional

Learning in the 21st Century
How to Connect, Collaborate, and Create

How to Work and Homeschool
Practical Advice, Tips, and Strategies from Parents

Educating Your Gifted Child
How One Public School Teacher Embraced Homeschooling

Coming Soon from GHF Press

www.giftedhomeschoolers.org/ghf-press/

Pamela Price

Gifted, Bullied, Resilient

Corin Goodwin and Mika Gustavson

Writing Your Own Script: A Parent's Role in the Gifted Child's Social Development

Jade Rivera

Microschooling

Bob Yamtich

Communicating with Gifted/2e Kids

Self-Directed Learning:
Documentation and Life Stories

By Wes Beach

Edited by Sarah J. Wilson

Published by GHF Press
A Division of Gifted Homeschoolers Forum
3701 Pacific Ave. SE - PMB #609
Olympia, WA 98501

ISBN-13: 978-0692407615 (GHF Press)
ISBN-10: 0692407618

Rosie Lakos' and Micah Harmon's stories, "Discarding Assumptions," and "Are Goals Important?" have appeared in altered form in previous issues of *The Homeschooler*, the HomeSchool Association of California's quarterly magazine.

Cover design by Shawn Keehne.
www.shawnkeehne.com • skeehne@mac.com

Dedication

This book is dedicated to the fifteen hundred graduates of Beach High School. They have taught me a huge amount about the incredible range of human talent and potential.

Table of Contents

Acknowledgments

I am grateful to the same GHF folks and other colleagues I named in the acknowledgments in my first GHF Press book—you know who you are.

I am deeply indebted to each person who took the time to share their stories, the stories that appear in this book, and also to those people who allowed me to include their college application documents herein. In some cases I had not been in touch with these people for many years, and it was a pleasure to get caught up with them.

I also owe thanks to every student I've worked with during the past 54 years, in public schools, a private one, and my own Beach High School. Each one has influenced my work.

In an inverted way, I am grateful for my 31 years in the public schools. My experiences in them led me to see, finally, better ways of supporting young people in growing and learning.

Sally Bracho was a student I knew well in the late 1960s; we reconnected in 2010. I've thought a lot about a comment she made in a note on a 2014 Christmas card: "I have the feeling that I'm finally at the top of my game, just as I face the downhill side of life—very odd to be in that position." Whether or not I'm at the top of my game, I've realized, thanks to Sally, that I'm not at the bottom of the hill.

My wife Judy Hubbard is a constant source of realization.

Editor's Note

In the interest of showing exactly what Beach High School students and their parents submitted to colleges and universities, any errors in the original transcripts have been left unedited and unmarked. Students' stories, however, have been edited in the interest of space and clarity. Those edits are not indicated.

Any editing errors in the remainder of the book are my own.

Sarah J. Wilson
Editor

Introduction

My high school years were a waste of time, at least academically. I received all A's (except for one B, the result of a conflict with an English teacher) with little effort and experienced essentially no intellectual stimulation. After graduation I went to UCLA and was shocked by the demands placed on me. I started as a pre-med major, but decided after my first set of finals (the biggest shock) that I would become a teacher and try to change things.

Over the course of 32 years, I taught in two public junior high schools, a K-8 private free school, a K-8 public school, and two public high schools. I never felt a complete sense of belonging in any of these schools, although I worked hard to teach in ways that made sense to me. I wanted to empower students. But my ways became increasingly unacceptable to the people who ran the schools. A principal who one year wanted to nominate me as state teacher of the year did a 180-degree turn the next year and began to write negative evaluations of my work; these evaluations included some skewed perceptions and violated my contract. Eventually, I felt it necessary to take my attorney with me to meetings with school and district administrators to defend myself. This was the last straw. I resigned and began working full time through Beach High School (BHS), my private high school (nothing more than a home office), which I had set up ten years earlier. (Conflict of interest was one of the charges against me.)

What I saw increasingly during my time in the public schools was students being lied to, manipulated, and ignored as individuals with unique strengths and talents, burdened with and sometimes damaged by a one-size-fits-all rigid and narrow curriculum.

A BHS graduate, Rosey, who had asked to graduate early, recently emailed me. What she wrote illustrates what I observed in public schools.

> While I was attending Middlebay High School* I became very unhappy. I felt trapped and didn't even know who I was anymore. I felt foreign and unfamiliar to even my own thoughts, voice, and mind. I also felt incredibly drained physically, my health was weak and I was sick a lot. (*Read Chapter 3 to learn how Rosey found a much better situation for herself.*)

Beach High School serves young people like Rosey who do not believe that a traditional high school education is what they want or need. BHS students often graduate shortly after enrolling, sometimes at 14 or 15 or 16 years old, not because they have completed high-school coursework, but on the basis of their readiness to move on with their lives and their maturity and personal strengths, which are described on a BHS transcript. Others stay enrolled for months or years, engaging in endeavors of their choice. They, too,

---

*The name of the high school has been changed.

graduate with a diploma and a transcript showing their achievements. BHS graduates have accomplished a great deal in the trades, the arts, business, and the professions, and they often reach the highest levels of formal education. Their recognition of their genuine interests and talents and their self-knowledge, confidence, enthusiasm, determination, ability to persevere, and sense of autonomy carry them where they want to go.

I was angry way too often while working in the public schools, and I can still become very angry when I hear of a student who has been very badly treated in school. But more important, my work brings me a wonderful sense of well-being. When I am in the midst of an active, ongoing conversation with a student that will lead to her or his escape from a constraining and limiting "educational" situation and open a path on which she or he can, as Rosey says, "make her own educational choices and create a life on her own terms," I feel, sinking into my very center and also rising up from it, an enveloping sense of purpose, meaning, buoyancy, fulfillment, and joy.

The aim of this book is to share my experiences with you so that you can support kids you care about in creating experiences during their teen years that will provide the foundation for productive and fulfilling adult lives.

Chapter 1

Nontraditional Ways to Spend the "High School" Years

Unschooling is defined in many ways. In my view, a teen is an unschooler if she is free to choose how she spends her time. I believe that all people learn continuously, regardless of what they're doing, so I don't include in this definition "how she spends her time in educational activities." Since all Beach High School students are free to direct their own education, all are unschoolers, even when they *choose* to participate in formal, traditional schooling.

But this book is not just for unschoolers. Its contents should be useful regardless of whether you're considering homeschooling that resembles traditional education, the most radical unschooling, or something in between.

Because of California's very limited regulation of homeschoolers, homeschooling of any variety is easy in this state. Laws may be more restrictive in other states, but there are unschoolers in every state. Homeschooling parents in your state and local groups and networks are sources of the necessary information about how to support homeschooling and unschooling (see *Resources*).

Evan Byrne submitted a wonderfully detailed essay when he wanted to graduate from Beach High School. I include an edited version here because I think it describes very well how and why one person decided against traditional schooling and instead pursued his interests and passions.

To best elaborate on the areas required for this essay, I will summarize my life since I left formal school. I am a passion-oriented person and I have learned the majority of my skills by pursuing my various passions in some way, shape, or form.

The last school I attended was Oak Grove School in Ojai, California. School was very stressful and frustrating for me. I had trouble concentrating on many subjects because I had no interest in learning them. The subjects I performed best in were subjects I enjoyed. At 10 years old, I had difficulty finding a functional use for things like algebra. I left after completing the fourth grade and began a somewhat formal homeschooling routine; however, much of the work still seemed pointless to me as it was much of the same material, but now I had the added distraction of the things I actually wanted to do at home. I found it hard to concentrate on and put any real effort toward something I had no interest in. It was not until these seemingly pointless subjects applied to my interests that I learned them, and quite easily.

I had always loved to fly model airplanes with my father when I was younger, but it was the free time I had after leaving school that really led me to pursue them on my own. I owned a model of just about every type: gas, electric, sailplane, free flight, etc. I loved to build models

1

with my dad, which led to my designing and building my own models from scratch. I would often call upon resources like NACA's (now NASA) airfoil database while designing wings which I would later use on my own models. Model building gave me lots of experience in crafting, construction, using tools, adhesives, and covering materials. As I began to discover the depth of the internet, I began using online forums to research and collect construction techniques, design ideas, and opinions from individuals who shared this passion. As a major component in the designing of any aircraft is weight, I began researching the weights of the electrical components I would be installing in my models to try to decrease weight and increase performance. This became one of my first practical uses for math. Many calculations were required, from the accumulative weights of building materials to push arm lengths. I would often go to my parents for a small math lesson if I needed to understand an aspect of my construction or design. One equation that I memorized very early on that later came into heavy use when I started learning to fly "full scale" airplanes was the following: (weight x arm = moment, total moment / total weight = CG location aft of datum). This is crucial to determining how an airplane will perform, as well as ensuring the aircraft is safe to fly.

Within two years of leaving school, I began the sport of unicycling. I had always enjoyed being active, especially riding bikes, but I wanted something more unique and difficult to learn. I was really seeking a steep and long learning curve. Unfortunately, I learned how to ride in about two days. To increase the difficulty, I again went online and discovered the sport of "extreme unicycling." This involved doing just about anything you would see a professional biker or skater do, but on a unicycle, such as jumping staircases, grinding rails, riding skate parks, and riding mountain bike trails. The sport was rather "underground" at the time, and due to the lack of people in my area that participated in the sport, my main access to new information, videos, tutorials, parts shops, and general networking came through the internet.

Online discussion groups were already very useful to me with model airplanes, and unicycling was no different. I loved the ability to get feedback from many sources rapidly, and to share the knowledge I was acquiring with others. This led to a very extensive knowledge of computer use, researching, and online sales. I bought and sold unicycles from individuals using money orders and online payments. Unicycling was also the start of my passion for videography, which I still enjoy today. I would routinely film new tricks and compile that footage with a soundtrack using a video editing program and post them on the discussion boards for people's comments and critiques. Unicycling gave me a purpose for building upon the minimal skill I had with my family's welder. I received many tips and tricks from a well-known metal craftsman at my local airport, and began making various components out of metal I ordered from an aircraft-metal-supply. I would periodically sell my components to fellow unicyclists because my components took into account current equipment wants and needs by top people in the sport. Unicycling taught me the importance of seeking like-minded individuals for support and furthering my expertise in whatever area interests me.

When I was 14 years old, I started taking sailplane lessons at a nearby sailplane port. My parents have always been immersed in aviation so it was all very familiar to me, as I had essentially grown up at an airport. Though I hadn't previously shown an interest in learning to fly, a simple two-minute scene from the movie *The Thomas Crown Affair* spawned my curiosity.

It was this initial curiosity that later formed my life as it stands today. Just after reaching the minimum of 10 hours instruction required, I made my first glider solo. This was an amazingly liberating experience, and my interest in all forms of aviation skyrocketed. My father suggested learning to fly my family's 1946 Piper J3 Cub, which is referred to as a "taildragger" and is considered more difficult and responsive than a traditional Cessna-type trainer. This was right up my alley. Due to my recent glider experience, I soloed the Cub very quickly, and began flying it on a nearly daily basis. I went beyond just learning what was required to perform standard operations to learning aerobatics, short field operations, and formation flying with a close friend of mine, Sam Mason (BHS graduate). In 2007 and 2008, I was awarded the Youngest Pilot Award at the National West Coast Piper Cub Fly-In in Lompoc, California.

When it came time to study and take the tests required to receive my private pilot's license, I realized how much my previous experience in model aircraft would pay off. My knowledge of aerodynamics already spanned much further than the material required, which is often a difficult area for student pilots. I also already knew how to perform a weight and balance check (used on most preflight inspections) due to my model aircraft experience. I received my private pilot's license in 2008, followed by my instrument rating in 2009, and my commercial license in 2010, which allowed me to begin flying for hire.

On May 15, 2010, while I was flying home in my parents' J-3 Piper Cub from a day of skydiving in Lompoc, I experienced an engine failure. In about 70 seconds, I cycled through my emergency procedures, located a local middle school underneath me with a minimal number of people, set up a landing approach, and landed in a 650-foot long school field. Little to my knowledge, I had landed in about a 20-25 mph tailwind, and thus had used up the entire length of the grass field and spun 180 degrees before coming to a stop. The landing gear had broken off the airplane, the propeller was folded back, and the left wing was damaged. Fortunately, I was uninjured. This was a very powerful experience for me. Never in my wildest dreams did I think that I would be using all those emergency procedures that student pilots are taught while getting their license, much less when I was only 18. An investigation by the NTSB and a local mechanic determined that a partially clogged fuel line and poor fuel siphon caused the engine failure. This experience really opened my eyes to the dangers and possibilities of the world I live in. This has increased my personal safety level when flying, as well as has led me to encourage other people to take precautions to avoid the situation I was forced to deal with.

My father owns an aerial photography business that he operates with our airplanes. As I gained experience, I began flying photo missions. This became an excellent opportunity for me to fly and earn money. As the business began to grow into the need for larger cameras, more cameras, bigger areas and wider coverage (entire west coast), the talk of an additional airplane came about. We obtained a Piper Aztec, which presented me with a need to obtain my multi-engine rating. In 2011, I added on my multi-engine rating to my already large list of ratings, given my age.

In early July 2011, I began working for Aviad Aerial Advertising, a sky-billboard towing company. Due to the small nature of the company, each pilot was essentially in charge of his own operation. From shipping coordination with the banner manufacturer, communications with airport officials, and scheduling maintenance for the airplanes, to cleaning and performing oil changes on the company vehicle, this was an incredible learning experience. Needless to say, aviation has been an amazing, powerful, and extremely beneficial influence on my life, from flying 747 simulators and flying biplanes upside down, to conversing with aeronautical engineers and airline pilots. Due to the nature of aviation, many of the people I am surrounded by are much older than I, which I believe has contributed to my maturity at a young age. Aviation has introduced me to many knowledgeable and passionate people.

In 2009, I began the sport of bodybuilding. I began going to a local gym and absolutely fell in love. Initially, I was just interested in the exercise portion, but later learned that diet and overall lifestyle played as large or larger a role than what I did in the gym. I began to read nutrition and training articles on a daily basis, gathering as much information as I could to help facilitate maximal muscle gain, while increasing my overall health. I was consistent and motivated, and my previous experience with online research gave me a tremendous ability to find and decipher information. I kept diet and training logs. I had each meal planned and built according to my nutritional needs. I noticeably changed my entire physique over the course of two years. I also became accustomed to various sorts of social disapproval due to my odd lifestyle and this I believe has given me the ability to keep a better focus on my goals in the face of social pressures.

After having seen Sanjay Gupta's *The Last Heart*, I was intrigued by the diet information which seemed contradictory to all the information I had been reading for years on bodybuilding websites. I set out to disprove this information for myself to further rationalize my current diet. At the time I was consuming high amounts of animal products. It was this research that caused the largest change in my life. I was further motivated by the fact that my entire family history is plagued with common diseases. My father had colon cancer, as did his father. My mother's father died from complications from a bypass, and my 45-year-old uncle had a heart attack and a stent put in. I had just stumbled upon the information that could enable me to essentially ensure I would never have to face these diseases, as well as drastically improve my quality of life and longevity. This information was so exciting that I began thinking of making a career of it.

I am currently studying to obtain my NASM (National Academy of Sports Medicine) Certified Personal Trainer Certificate. I intend to combine my love of fitness with my desire to help people better their own health and physique. I would like to obtain my A.A. in athletic training or nutrition, though I feel I can obtain far more valuable information outside of school, so I may take that route rather slowly. I currently work at a local organic farm and have been immersing myself in sustainable agriculture literature. I am constructing my own mini-farm at home to supply my family with food, and I plan to eventually sell produce of my own.

Why do I deserve a high school diploma? I deserve a diploma because all these combined experiences have left me with the resourcefulness and gumption to not only excel at the things I am passionate about, but make a living doing them. When I need help along the way, I am exceptionally capable of seeking out the information I require and implementing that information to better myself and achieve my goals.

If Evan were to decide, for example, that he wanted to go to medical school in pursuit of his interest in health, there's nothing stopping him. Evan could enter a community college (see Chapter 3), build a solid record, transfer to a four-year college or university, and go on to medical school. Some of my students have done exactly this. On the other hand, Evan could build a productive life in many ways without ever setting foot on a college campus. Some of my students have created productive and fulfilling lives for themselves without earning a college degree. You'll read the stories of some people who didn't go to college in Chapter 6. Right now, here's Smith Dobson's story.

My experience with public education leading up to high school had been a rough one, full of detours—experimental safe havens for a child having difficulty adapting to the format. It was a challenge for me to relate to other kids. Teachers were mostly seen as frightening authoritarians, robbing me of the freedoms I had back at home.

I grew up in a close-knit family of musicians, my mother and father both playing professionally. I had big dreams, or dreams of being big, in my early years. Every time my parents left for a gig, I would cry, not so much because I was sad to see them go, but because I wanted to be on the gig with them. I wanted to earn the respect of my older contemporaries and be treated as an equal. I wanted to be rewarded with the same level of independence.

I started playing drums at age two; I just crawled up to a drum set and started exploring. My parents were as supportive as parents can be. They never forced me to learn music, just reacted to my interest in it, which I think is a great approach to take with kids. It was the same for my sister. We both developed independently into professional musicians.

As a child, if something piqued my interest in a heartfelt way, nothing would stop me from pursuing it. I tended to thrive in subjects where I felt my creativity took part in the process of discovery. Teachers, of course, helped a great deal, as long as they were sensitive enough to recognize this. It was when the learning process became "required" that I tended to falter. I had a genuine lack of interest in certain subjects, which became exacerbated by poor grades. I developed a crippling fear of failing in these subjects, which only further stifled the process of learning them.

By fourth grade, I was becoming emotionally unstable. This fear of being forced to learn subjects that I struggled in, like math, was taking its toll on me. I would show up to class, see a long-division problem on the chalkboard (our day's math assignment), and burst into tears as we sang the Pledge of Allegiance. It was a mess. My teacher thought I was being abused by my parents, which I wasn't. I had a fear of being kept after class and she kept me after class constantly, thinking she was helping. By the beginning of fifth grade, my parents were getting desperate for some other option. Public school had become a prison that caused me nothing but anxiety and depression.

A friend of my parents had suggested a different kind of school, the Monarch Community School, which was essentially a hippie commune. Each grade, kindergarten through sixth, studied in the same room. Remarkably, this close proximity actually worked pretty well for the students. That short period at Monarch was a relatively happy one in my childhood. After Monarch, I reluctantly tried junior high. By the beginning of eighth grade, I was pulled out again and homeschooled for the rest of that year.

My father was more of a traditionalist than my mom in some ways, and was never really in favor of my pursuing alternate forms of education. But he was also a good man. When he saw me depressed or in distress, he addressed it, rather than pretending that his young son was like everyone else's kid. Nevertheless, when it came time to approach the idea of high school, he was strongly in favor of my trying it out. I wanted to show my old man that I was big and strong and courageous like him, so I went into high school with that kind of optimism.

At first, it seemed as though high school might actually be something new and different. It was much bigger and crammed full of students, and this made it sort of exciting. For the first couple months, the kids seemed envious of my ability as a musician, but that envy quickly soured to jealousy, then to ugly adolescent spite. My withdrawn, awkward nature didn't help win anyone over. Eventually, high school became so horrific that instead of enjoying my lunch break, I would walk home. When I arrived home, my mom, surprised to see me, would ask if I was OK. I could only answer her by breaking down in tears, slumped over my bed.

It was during this period that, just by chance, I happened to sign up for Life Science class, an introductory class in one of my worst subjects. I quickly became fascinated by the unorthodox style of our teacher, Wes Beach. With his white beard and casual demeanor, he seemed less like a science teacher and more like a character out of a Melville novel. Wes encouraged us to refer to him by his first name. Our only real assignment was to write a response to what he'd written on sheets of paper which he passed out at the beginning of class. It could be as short as one sentence or as long as several pages. Once we were finished with that, we were more or less free to do as we pleased.

I took this writing assignment seriously, inadvertently using it as an opportunity to pour out my frustrations with the claustrophobia I was experiencing at the time. One day, Wes asked me to chat after class. "I've been reading your writing and think it's very good," he said, surprising me. (It hadn't occurred to me that he might actually read the stuff.) He went on, "I also want to tell you, if you're feeling frustrated with any part of the education you're receiving here, if you are strong in an area like music, but don't feel like the music program is very good here, then perhaps you should study somewhere else."

Of course, I was shocked to hear this from an adult high school teacher. Wes explained my options, about taking the CHSPE* or the GED† and perhaps going to college early. The idea of my doing this seemed inconceivable, in terms of talking my father into it; however, I had reached a dark point of no resolve with high school. When I declared feeling "suicidal" to my mother, she found a way to convince my father.

My life improved in every way imaginable after I left high school. Enrolling at Cabrillo College [a community college] seemed to answer all my problems. Students were friendlier, as they had more or less made it out of the terrors of adolescence. For the first time in my life, I had a set of friends who were fellow musicians near my age group. I stayed on board with subjects that I struggled in, like math, but my fear of failure was beginning to subside a bit. Cabrillo had a superb music program, and I took advantage of this as much as possible. I also took classes in literature, creative writing, acting, art history, and art.

---

*The CHSPE is the California High School Proficiency Exam, which, when passed, yields a high-school-diploma-equivalent certificate.
†The GED is the General Educational Development test, which, when passed, certifies the test-taker has American or Canadian high-school-level academic skills.

Currently, at 37, I am a professional musician and composer, having lived for the past 15 years in the San Francisco Bay Area. I also paint and write. Essentially, I'm still practicing the same things that I was interested in as a kid. My latest venture has been to learn the saxophone, which had always been a dream of mine. I didn't quite have the self-discipline to learn the sax as a child, but around the age of 23 I decided to try in earnest. I started hanging out in the practice rooms of San Francisco State University with a rented saxophone, picking up whatever I could from students and teachers. Some of the professors, who were also friends of mine, even gave me the nickname "street faculty."

I think it's important to be fearless when educating one's self, to embrace what is truly in the heart. I reject the notion that we essentially stop learning at a certain point during adulthood. If one suffers this fate, I blame the pressures society places on us, not our own brains. I've seen it happen over and over again: college graduates in a state of panic because they suddenly realize they've been conditioned to spend their entire education pursuing the myth of "choosing a career." Suddenly, their heart isn't in the path they've chosen, or been chosen for them. Motivated only by the existential fear of being faced with adulthood, they begrudgingly stick to these careers.

I feel truly blessed that, because of parents who were sensitive to my needs, and because of key individuals, like Wes Beach, who steered me in a safe direction where my interests could be properly developed, I am still developing them today.

Evan's story illustrates spending one's "high school" years immersed in not a traditional curriculum, but exploring genuine interests. Smith simply skipped three years of high school and went on to a community college. It's also entirely possibly for a teen who knows he wants to go directly to a four-year college to choose both traditional and nontraditional learning experiences that will make reaching this goal possible. These experiences can include independent learning at home; work with tutors and mentors; special programs sponsored by schools or other organizations; high school courses taken in public, private, and distance learning schools; community college and university coursework; volunteer work; travel; and training programs and employment.

In Chapter 4, we'll review entire and partial transcripts of four people to see how they prepared for and succeeded in gaining admission to four-year colleges and universities.

Chapter 2
Finding a Life (not Necessarily a Lifetime) Direction

Are Goals Important?

In articles, books, and conversations, as well as from other sources, one often reads or hears of the importance of consistently having goals and working toward them. I don't buy it.

I'm not denying that setting goals and persevering in reaching them is sometimes useful or even of critical importance. But I don't believe that having goals is always necessary in a fulfilling and productive life.

When I was a junior in high school I wrote a term paper on brain surgery, and as a result decided to become a doctor. I graduated, entered UCLA, and declared a pre-med major, an available major at the time. But when I reached my first finals and realized that I would be taking three-hour exams, each of which would demand a mastery of an entire semester's subject matter, I faced academic demands far beyond anything I had experienced in high school. I concluded, in fact, that high school had been a waste of time, academically at least. I decided to become a teacher and try to change things.

After I earned my B.A. and while still working on a teaching credential, I obtained my first job, teaching science in a junior high school in Los Angeles. I remained there for five-and-a-half years, during which I read *Summerhill* and then began reading the standard bibliography on open education, books by John Holt, Jonathan Kozol, Paul Goodman, Edgar Friedenberg, and others. James Herndon's *How To Survive in Your Native Land* became the book I returned to again and again when I was frustrated or angry about something that was going on at school.

I had not adopted a goal of becoming radicalized when I picked up *Summerhill,* but this was the result.

There were other twists and turns in my 32 years in public and private schools, none of which appeared as a result of pursuing goals. I won't use up my allotted space trying to describe all of them, but a few deserve mention.

Many years ago, I read in the local newspaper (I was then teaching in a public high school in Santa Cruz County, California) of a group that was picketing the San Luis Obispo County (California) Office of Education because school officials were harassing homeschoolers. I figured that any group that was doing such a thing was worth learning about. I discovered that the group was part of the HomeSchool Association of California (HSC), and that the president of HSC lived in San Jose, not far from my home. I called her up, set a time to visit, drove to her house, and had a very engaging conversation with her. The next thing I knew I was writing articles for HSC's magazine, *The California HomeSchooler,* the precursor of *The Homeschooler,* and not long after that I was invited to join HSC's board, on which I served for two years. HSC supported me in giving talks all over California and in speaking at HSC's annual conference. I became known in the homeschooling community and was invited to speak in other states.

I love my roles as writer, speaker, and supporter of homeschooling, but none of these roles was the result of having set goals. What they did result from was having pursued my deep interest in education since my freshman year at UCLA 57 years ago, being open to learning from my experiences, and creating a path step by step.

During the last ten years I worked in public schools, I ran a program for "gifted and talented" students. One of these students, Debbie, wanted to take the California High School Proficiency Exam, earn the high-school-diploma-equivalent certificate awarded upon passing the exam, and leave high school early. Her parents encouraged her to stick it out and graduate from high school because they felt the memories would be important. However, they did allow her to take part-time classes at the local community college. Several years later she called me, and we set up a time to have breakfast together and get caught up. During our conversation she told me she was about to enter a Ph.D. program in aerospace physiology. "Wow," I said, "that's an unusual field. Where did your interest in it come from?" She said, with all seriousness, "From watching *Top Gun*." She hadn't bought her movie ticket looking for academic guidance, but she found it. She then did set a goal, not as a consequence of looking for one, but as a result of watching a movie about people performing complex tasks at high altitudes. As I said at the beginning, I'm not arguing against goal-setting, but I do believe that it's fine to live some parts of one's life without significant goals, and that openness to experience is more important sometimes than having clear goals.

Debbie did earn her Ph.D., studying the effects of working in space and in fast jets. She joined the navy and was assigned to work with submariners. You may have laughed when you read this, and I did too when I first heard it. But when you stop and think about it, submariners, just like people flying planes, are working in conditions different from those at the surface of the Earth.

When a goal is set and then reached—earning a college degree, traveling around the world, obtaining a desired job—it doesn't necessarily mean that anything is settled for the long term. When my wife was in high school, her doctor decided he didn't want to continue working in medicine, moved to a different part of the state, and became a potter. One of my former students spent years working in communications, tired of it, and changed direction. You'll read her story later in this chapter.

A substantial number of psychologists agree that there are five major components of personality: openness to experience is one of them (to find the others, do a search for "personality big five"). Some people are more open to experience than others, but everyone is to some extent. Openness can assist in discovering life's possibilities.

A Passion for Surfing Leads to Successful Businesses

In 1987 my wife-to-be and I wandered into a women's clothing shop, Oceania Imports, in Capitola, California, a beach town close to where we now live. We immediately saw a dress we both liked and it became my wife's wedding dress. While she was trying it on, I got to talking with Chuck Heppner, the owner, was interested in what he said, offered to take him to lunch, and he accepted; he told me his story during that lunch. He went to high school and did very well, but after graduation decided to pursue his passion—surfing—and to travel instead of going to college. He spent four years exploring the world. On Bali it occurred to him that some of the beautiful objects he saw there could be purchased, taken elsewhere, and sold for a profit. This was the beginning of the path that led to his opening his clothing store. In 1987, he not only owned the store but also a facility on Bali where most of the clothing he sold was manufactured. He hadn't gone to college but had taken a few practical classes such as accounting at Cabrillo College, the local community college.

While in Capitola recently, I went into Oceania and discovered that Chuck no longer spent time there; his wife Jill managed the store. She told me that Chuck had started a new business, so I set up a time with him to learn about it.

The two of them opened a clothing store in Hawaii, then another, but business was not good after 9/11 and the Great Recession, and these two stores closed. Searching for something else to work on, Chuck came upon some stone in Indonesia that he realized could be made into tile. He began working with a partner, and Island Stone was created. Island Stone North America now employs 300 people in Indonesia and 25 in Santa Cruz, California, where Chuck has his office and a call center, and where display boards are created to send to the 600 Island Stone outlets in the U.S. and Canada, supplied by four warehouses across the U.S.

Chuck Heppner spent little time in college and does not have a degree, but has nevertheless created two highly successful businesses. He has no regrets about not having obtained a degree, but his advice to others is, "If you don't have a passion, go to college."

Jill Heppner went from high school to California Polytechnic State University, San Luis Obispo, where she majored in architecture. She was not happy there, returned to Santa Cruz County, and studied nutrition at Cabrillo College. Changing direction again, she transferred to San Francisco State University and graduated with honors and a degree in marketing. She says her studies were interesting but are only minimally relevant in the work that she now does.

Another Perspective on College

I've gotten to know a checker at the supermarket where my wife and I do a lot of shopping. I'll call her Miriam. She went to high school, was minimally engaged in her studies, and thought at the time, and still thinks, that her courses were not very useful. After a short stay at a community college, she left and did not return to higher education, but she has been a serious reader since she was a young girl and believes she is as well educated in literature and history as a person with a four-year degree.

After high school, Miriam moved from Virginia to California, worked in retail sales for a while, and then took a job where she learned the skills of a graphic artist when those skills involved paper and paste.

Miriam took time off to have children, and when she went back to work she entered the grocery business and has remained in it for the past 23 years. The job of checker is physically demanding, and, at 61, she's not sure how long she can continue. She struggles financially.

Miriam has a son who is now in college, and she urges him to persist at his studies until he earns a degree. When I asked her what she would do differently if she had her life to live over, I was surprised that she didn't say she would go to college. What she did say was that she would have become much more secure had she returned to work in graphics and learned to do the work with computers. I asked her what she would say about living life if she were speaking to a group of teens, and she said she'd tell them to keep seeking knowledge, and, if they didn't go to college, to learn a trade that would provide a good income.

In Chapter 7 you'll read about Micah Harmon, who systematically sought out a trade that is providing him with a good income.

An Art Student Becomes a Doctor

As I was working on this book, I had a kidney stone attack and wound up in the ER at a local hospital. There I was attended to by Dr. Jeremy Orvik; it appeared that the staff called him Jeremy, not Dr. Orvik. After he got my pain under control, and making sure Jeremy had time for a conversation, I indulged my penchant for talking to people about their work and their lives. Jeremy was quite open. One thing he told me was that he chose to attend the Virginia Commonwealth University School of Medicine for two reasons: it was inexpensive, and it was close to the ocean, so he could go surfing. When I asked him why he went into medicine, he said it was a long story, but gave me the short version. I asked him to tell me more at another time; he readily agreed and gave me his phone number. After a nearly three-weeks-long game of phone tag, we connected. (In his outgoing voicemail message, he says, "I'm either workin', sleepin', or surfin'.") Here's the story he told me.

He grew up in Danville, across the bay from San Francisco. His father was a self-made man who had built major shopping malls but fell on hard times and died when Jeremy was 16. This was deeply affecting and created financial uncertainty, so Jeremy shouldered some of the responsibility for himself and his family and took on jobs. After graduating from high school, he entered the University of California, Santa Cruz; he was interested in photography and declared an art major. But he saw that most of his fellow students weren't devoted to their studies and were instead drinking, getting high, having sex, and skipping classes. He became disillusioned and discouraged; he took long hikes into the woods surrounding the university campus. Returning from one of these hikes and heading to a class, he heard a very clear, insistent voice conveying the most essentially important message he's ever heard: "Become a doctor." Jeremy considers himself to be a spiritual person but not a religious one, and does not attach religious significance to this voice. But it was powerful. (In his book, *Hallucinations,* Oliver Sacks says that hearing voices is not terribly uncommon and is not usually a sign of psychosis.)

He decided that becoming a doctor would be the best way to make good use of his life and to serve others. He went to the biology department office and asked what he needed to do to prepare for medical school. The secretary asked if he had taken physics or chemistry, and he said no. So he developed plans to change his course and graduated with a degree in biology. Wanting to make sure that medicine was the right vocation for him, he spent four years training and working as an EMT and a paramedic. Settled on medicine as a career, he completed medical school in Virginia and a residency in southern California. He then came to Santa Cruz to treat people with kidney stones and other maladies that require immediate attention.

A Change in Direction After College

YunJoo Kim left high school after one semester, attended a community college, transferred to San Francisco State University, and graduated at 18 with a bachelor's degree in Radio and Television, New Media Emphasis. She tells the rest of her story this way:

I was extremely fortunate to have landed a job just a couple of months out of college. Instead of having to resort to waiting tables, I was positioned at a high tech company in San Francisco as a videographer and editor. It was a huge challenge, working long hours, and traveling about 80% of the time. Not only was that exciting for me at that age, but it fueled me to deepen my skill set. It wasn't long before I was rising up the corporate latter and relocating to Los Angeles for a new position with a much higher salary. I felt extremely fortunate to have had the opportunity to experience the dotcom boom and all the perks that companies offered at that time. Going for a run on my lunch break, having catered lunches provided, creating my own flexible hours, and having company BBQs every Friday was just an example of an average workweek. But I also experienced the flipside to the boom.

It was 2001 and I was working in Los Angeles and New York City as an interactive producer. The tragedy of 9/11 happened and something deep woke up inside of me. Experiencing this tragedy on an intimate level made me question my purpose and inquire about how fulfilling my work was. On a deeper level, I realized the work had become more of a daily grind, which wasn't making a large impact in people's lives. Yes, maybe I was making businesses and large Fortune 500 corporations make or exceed their projections each quarter while keeping profits high and losses low. That just wasn't sitting well with me. I had lost a bit of faith in the industry and needed to reassess.

During this stressful time of transition, I took up a lot of yoga and massage for my own self-care. I felt more grounded and less stressed from the traveling and computer work. That simply wasn't enough. It was time to make a conscious decision to choose a different and more fulfilling path. I decided to take a yoga teacher training course and I went to massage school. This was a huge shift into uncertain territory. I thoroughly enjoyed being a student again and immersing myself in subjects that were about healing. My intention was to deepen my own knowledge for my personal practice and not necessarily to become a practitioner. However, as I continued to take more courses and trainings I realized what a profound impact it had on my own health and well-being. I wanted to share this with others.

This was the beginning of a new career as a massage and yoga therapist. For several years, I worked full-time in private practice as well as in spas, integrative medicine centers, and yoga studios. It felt so natural and effortless to work in the healing arts. My business background also helped me to establish a practice quickly and successfully. I worked with physicians, psychologists, and other healthcare providers in an integrative and holistic setting, helping others on their healing path. I had a high-profile clientele including many celebrities. I felt incredibly fortunate to be successful once again and in a field that brought me deep joy and fulfillment. I had finally come to the realization that being in service of others truly was my life's purpose.

After being a massage and yoga therapist for eight years, it was time to deepen my knowledge in a field that had always fascinated me, Chinese medicine. Growing up with my grandmother, I was exposed to herbology at an early age. The herbs she would brew in the kitchen would smell up the entire house. It wasn't my fondest childhood memory; however, I remember the stories that went along with it. She would explain how these herbs helped to keep the cold and flu away or how they gave you more energy and vitality. It was at Five

Branches University in Santa Cruz, California, when I was reacquainted with these unusual smelling herbs with their medicinal powers. I committed to a 4+ year graduate program at the age of 30. This was the biggest challenge yet, especially after working in industry for so many years, just to find myself back to being a struggling student. It was a major life change and a huge bite of humility.

In the end, I knew the hard work and dedication would pay off. The vast field of Chinese medicine is beyond what words can write. With a 5000-year-old history, there is so much richness and knowledge that one can only chip away at in a lifetime. For this, I am grateful. With my previous careers, I always hit a plateau. It would get routine and repetitive. Even though massage and yoga were incredibly rewarding and service oriented, that too had its limits for growth. As a Chinese medicine practitioner, one becomes a student for life and for me that is priceless. I get to share this medicine and its ancient wisdom traditions with others so they can empower themselves to heal naturally and holistically. Through acupuncture, herbology, massage, diet and nutrition, and energy cultivation practices, this complete healing system is truly a gift to share. I have been fortunate to come into this medicine through my own healing. In a way, it found me and I am grateful to have many years ahead as a student, teacher, and practitioner and, most important, be of service to those around me.

Finding a Direction

At some point in your life you may have a conversation, read a book, travel, hear a voice, live through a disaster, or have some other experience that can open up possibilities. My suggestion to you about how to find a life direction (and to be prepared for changes in direction): Be fully engaged in your experiences, whether you're watching a movie, surfing, driving across the country, taking a hike, attending classes, or whatever else. Be aware of and pay attention to opportunities that appear in your path.

Chapter 3
Enrolling in a Community College

Most of the students I work with leave high school part way through it, skip it altogether, or complete homeschooling at an early age. Most of them want to go to college, but they have not completed the courses often necessary for admission to four-year schools. Community colleges have proven to be good places to start. After building a solid record, transferring from a community college to a four-year college or university is entirely possible (although extremely competitive at a few very selective schools such as Stanford and impossible at Princeton), and moving on to graduate or professional school can follow. Many hundreds of my students have followed this path with great success; a number of them have earned graduate degrees and entered the professions.

In California where I live and work, and in some other states*, a person need only be 18 or older for admission to a community college; there are no subject or high school diploma requirements. However, people not yet 18 need a diploma or an equivalent certificate. Since most of my of my students are younger than 18, I provide them with a diploma and transcript based not on coursework but simply on their desire to move on. I have come to believe that the foundation for success in school and in life is built of personal traits and circumstances. Young people who feel they have some control over their lives and can make their own decisions rather than follow someone else's agenda, who know themselves and their abilities well, and who are confident and can persevere are in the best position to be successful in learning and in life. This belief is expressed in the preamble of Torrey Glenn's transcript, which follows her narrative, below.

Torrey

Torrey Glenn's transcript is a good example of what I most often provide to my students who want to enter a community college. As you'll see, it's entirely narrative. It provided a way for Torrey to enter a California community college before she was 18. She tells the story of what followed:

> I went to Cabrillo College and studied philosophy, Spanish, and horticulture. I continued working as a bookkeeper. My then-boyfriend and I rented an apartment in downtown Santa Cruz. We married when I was 18. In retrospect, I recognize this marriage as a sort of "rebellion," because we so desperately wanted to be viewed as adults. Shortly afterward, we sold nearly everything we owned, bought a van, and drove to Mexico. We stayed there for four or five

---

*It is well beyond the scope of this book to describe the admission requirements of community colleges in all 50 states. The kind of transcript I show in this chapter may not be acceptable in your state, but the more traditional transcripts shown in Chapter 4 may be. Contact your local community college to learn their requirements. Investigate carefully.

months, living out of our van. We spent most of our time in Oaxaca, a city with an impressive mix of colonial and modern neighborhoods, and a very nice English lending library.

Upon return to the U.S., our van broke down while visiting a friend in Denver. So, we decided to stay there. We lived in Denver for two years. I worked as a nanny, then at a preschool co-teaching a class of four-year-olds. These two years were rather indulgent and unfocused, an incredibly hedonistic hiccup in an otherwise fairly focused life. All that hedonism certainly highlighted my desire for meaning and focus. After drinking all that wine, I realized I needed to go to UC Davis and get a degree in viticulture—horticulture blended with the cultured history of wine. We decided to return to California and "sneak" back into Cabrillo College as California residents [rather than paying out-of-state tuition elsewhere].

Once at Cabrillo, I learned that the prerequisites for UCD's viticulture and enology program were heavily weighted towards the enology component. This is a serious, hard-core science major! The Cabrillo academic counselor told me that I needed to take calculus, biology, chemistry, physics. It was a truly overwhelming list of courses. I cried. A lot. Then I got really angry. Then I started taking classes. My first chemistry class at Cabrillo was taught by Christy Vogel. I excelled in the course (I had always been an A student, so no surprise really) and when she announced that tutors were needed for the upcoming semester I applied for the job. I started working as a chemistry tutor, then I became a Supplemental Instruction Leader (a position similar to a T.A. where you lead weekly study sessions for the class), and generally found an incredibly supportive and exciting academic community at Cabrillo.

At some point I realized that I was really enjoying tutoring chemistry, and that I was good at it. Another important factor was that the Cabrillo College chemistry faculty felt, and still feels, like family! My organic chemistry teacher, Harry Ungar, became a friend and mentor. I had never "fit in" anywhere, but I felt completely at home there. The impact was tremendous. The Cabrillo MESA center [a study environment for math, science, and engineering students] was also important, as was my excellent study partner whom I met while leading supplemental instruction sections for general chemistry. He and I studied for hours and hours together. All of this was just so positive, in a way that I had never experienced. In response, I decided that I should study chemistry, get a master's degree, and teach chemistry at a community college. And that's exactly what I did.

I finished my lower division requirements at Cabrillo and earned an A.S. in chemistry. I transferred to UCSC [University of California, Santa Cruz] and earned a B.A. in chemistry, then an M.S. in chemistry. I continued student teaching while at UCSC. I worked as a T.A. for Physical Chemistry while I was still an undergrad. I loved T.A.-ing!

My first teaching assignment was as a part-timer at Cabrillo College in the fall of 2006. I finished my degree that December. I got a tenured faculty position at City College of San Francisco in the fall of 2007, where I remain today. The job involves far more life counseling than I had imagined, and I'm an odd person to be a mentor, but that has turned out to be a very satisfying part of the work. I teach an incredibly hard course at CCSF (I have my office stocked with tissues ready for post-exam counseling—even the guys cry), but somehow students still trust me and respect me and recommend me to their friends, so I must be doing something right. So, there you have it. I'm a community college chemistry teacher.

TRANSCRIPT

Name: Torrey Ann Glenn
Address: 478 Citrus Court
Cactus Heights, CA 48370
Phone: 555-037-8385
Birth Date: 4/12/79
Parent: [Name omitted]
Entered: 8/14/96
Graduated: 8/26/96

Beach High School

3635 Sevilla Drive
Soquel, CA 95073
831-462-5867 • beachhi@cruzio.com

Beach High School exists to support students who want to gain or have gained all or part of their education outside of a traditional high school setting. We award diplomas to students who convincingly present themselves as ready and able to move on beyond high school and who have established a direction for the next part of their lives. Our experience over many years has taught us that people succeed in wonderful ways, including through academic work in college, whenever they make deliberate, informed, and deeply personal decisions to move on. Our graduates have accomplished a great deal in practical crafts, the arts, business, and the professions, and they often reach the highest levels of formal education. Their successes do not depend on completion of academic coursework in high school. It is their recognition of their genuine interests and talents and their self-knowledge, confidence, enthusiasm, determination, ability to persevere, and sense of autonomy that carry them where they want to go.

The duration of Torrey's enrollment, shown above, was very short, but this transcript represents her lifetime experiences and accomplishments, with an emphasis on the past few years. We have graduated her on the basis of who she has become, and we believe that her strengths and talents, both inborn and acquired, will be foundational in her future achievements.

In applying for graduation, Torrey wrote: "When I entered high school three years ago I'd had an overwhelming passion for knowledge. I couldn't resist a used book store and loved reading anything from sci-fi to anthropology. Everything unknown was interesting. I'd follow strange chains linked by the smallest connections. Warhol would lead to Dali and Dali would lead to Crick and DNA (if you don't know the remote connection ask me sometime!). Education was synonymous for exploration in my mind. However, that curiosity of mine has almost been killed by high school. And although it could be defended as an attempt to save the 'cat,' quite the opposite has been accomplished. It seems that what should have been instilled by school—the passion to learn—has nearly been extinguished.

"[W]hen even my mother agrees that I should leave high school—I've had enough!"

Torrey told us that the final blow was reading and trying to enjoy the required book for her upcoming senior AP English class and then realizing that her enjoyment would be ruined by having to squeeze her thoughts into "the standardized five paragraph analytical essay. I've stood eyewitness to, and even partaken in, the murder of many masterful books." She won't do it again.

Torrey's three-year high school record shows an academic GPA of very nearly 4.0 and includes several honors classes and a special studies class. Torrey has demonstrated her capacity for continuing the same kind of work in college by earning an A in Elementary Physics at UCSC [the University of California, Santa Cruz].

She also wrote: "I can't say that I am aspiring towards any particular career or even a single educational plan. I'll take Cabrillo College as a starting point and see where I go from there. I'd like to let my life evolve and grow without the format and confines of a plan. I'd like to travel, speak Spanish fluently, own a cat, read a million books. Of course, I could sum it up by saying that my education will always continue (even if it's only the lessons of feline ownership). I have a passion for knowledge, and am concerned with its preservation. To me, that is a qualification [for graduation] better than anything else."

One of Torrey's high school teachers, a demanding academician, wrote: "This unassuming young woman was easily the best student in my three sections of junior year Intensive English at [Middleroad] High last year [1995-96]. Her very first paper immediately set Torrey apart. Her control of the language was exceeded only by the quality of her insight. Here was a thinking adult in my classroom. Subsequent work confirmed my first impressions and likewise showed me that this performance, putting Torrey's composition among the half dozen or so best within my entire career of 12 years as English teacher, was not merely the result of a vigorous and mature intellect. Torrey was also working very hard.

"Torrey's choices for outside readings as an honor student were sophisticated and ambitious and provided opportunity for her to shine in work that was entirely independent. Some of her papers I would have been quite happy to submit to a teacher as my own work. The quality of her work . . . demonstrated that Torrey was eminently qualified for a more high-powered environment."

We feel privileged to be able to provide a way for this highly intelligent, sensitive, and very talented young woman to move beyond what is for her a confining and destructive environment and to seek a new lease on life in general and academic life in particular. She is not only in a very good position to live life beyond high school; she must so live it if she is to thrive. We predict that, however Torrey's life evolves, there will be splendid results. She has easily met our graduation requirements, and accordingly she was awarded a diploma on August 26, 1996.

Signed:_____

Wes Beach, Director

Seal:

Date:_____

About Beach High School

Beach High School is one of several private schools offering high school enrollment in Santa Cruz County, California. BHS's specialty is in supporting kids for whom the traditional path does not work. The majority of my students enroll for a short period of time; compile a portfolio documenting their interests, strengths, talents, accomplishments, and goals; earn a diploma based on this portfolio; and move on. Students who remain enrolled at BHS for an extended period of time enroll in college classes and distance learning courses, set up tutorials, engage in community activities and independent learning, do volunteer work, travel, and work. I only occasionally provide individualized coursework; almost all credit is based on students' experiences elsewhere.

Graduates who choose an academic path most often enter a community college, frequently at age 14 or 15 or 16, where they do very well. The amount of academic coursework they've done at the high school level doesn't seem to matter; those who skip most or even all of high school do just as well as those who complete two or three years. I believe it is their personal strengths—confidence, curiosity, enthusiasm, realistic self-knowledge, capacity for wholehearted engagement, ability to persevere, and a sense of autonomy—that are foundational in their successes. These people typically transfer to four-year colleges and universities after a productive stay in a community college. A smaller number of BHS graduates enter a four-year college directly. My students have gained admission to several campuses of the University of California, including Berkeley and UCLA, many campuses of the California State University, Stanford, Rice, Columbia, NYU, MIT, Caltech, Reed, Marlboro, Swarthmore, Sarah Lawrence, the Rhode Island School of Design, California Institute of the Arts, the Berklee College of Music, and many other schools. They have won many academic honors and awards; a substantial number enter graduate school.

Other people start their own businesses, enter the job market, enroll in trade and vocational schools, embark on extensive travels, or immerse themselves in independent learning and research. One graduate has, through self-teaching, become an expert on butterflies and has arranged to do research with a professor at Southern Oregon University. At least two BHS graduates are professional athletes.

I also offer diplomas to adults who have lived successful lives and have gained much more than a high school education through life experience.

I have a California Lifetime Secondary Credential (technically a Life Diploma) and an M.A. in educational counseling. I worked for 32 years in public and private schools teaching in several subject areas and directing alternative programs in grades K-14. I taught at a local comprehensive public high school for the last 20 of these years. At this school I ran a program for gifted and talented students for 10 years (1980-1990), and my private school is essentially an expanded version of that program.

Beach High School opened in the fall of 1981, offering very limited services to an occasional student in a special situation. I devoted myself full time to BHS in February of 1993, although I promptly fell ill and was not up to full-time work until the fall of 1993. Until April of 1994, when I awarded the first BHS diploma, I enrolled people and helped them get where they wanted to go while they were waiting to take the California High School Proficiency Examination. When I started providing diplomas, almost everyone opted to earn a diploma rather than take the Exam. Since April of 1994 I have awarded (as of June, 2014) about 1,450 diplomas to people ranging in age from 13 to 57.

~Wes Beach, Director

Rosey

I mentioned Rosey Lakos in the introduction to this book, and promised to tell you her story. Rosey graduated from Beach High School the same year Torrey did, 1996. At that time she wrote:

> While I was attending [Middlebay] High School, I became very unhappy. I felt trapped and didn't even know who I was anymore. I felt foreign and unfamiliar to even my own thoughts, voice, and mind. I also felt incredibly drained physically, my health was weak and I was sick a lot.

In 2014 Rosey wrote this:

> I earned my diploma from BHS eighteen years ago. After graduating, I traveled through Europe visiting seven different countries and gained a much wider perspective on life. I attended community college, exploring a variety of subject matters that interested me while also obtaining my A.A. and working full time. It was during this time that I discovered my innate drive to express myself through photographic arts. I went on to transfer to California College of the Arts, receiving the Faculty Honors Scholarship based on my portfolio. I graduated with a B.F.A. in photography, Academic Honors, High Distinction, a network of support and a more developed sense of myself as an artist. I have worked as a photographer doing custom photo sessions, been commissioned to make large pieces for retail environments and created a traveling vintage-style photo booth. Most recently my work has been published in a German art magazine. I am currently living in the Bay Area, working in the photo department at *Wired* magazine and contemplating grad school. My decision to pursue my high school diploma through BHS was the catalyst for me to put my educational choices in my own hands and create my life on my own terms.

Torrey and Rosey both attended public high schools and left after their junior years. Many BHS students leave earlier. Some skip high school altogether, as my son Brian did (his story and the stories of a number of other people appear in my book *Forging Paths: Beyond Traditional Education,* also published by GHF Press). And many of my students have been homeschoolers who have followed paths similar to Torrey's and Rosey's. In increasing numbers, BHS graduates spend time away from formal schooling before completing college, but there have also been numbers of people who have gone straight to college and been very successful.

Questions and Answers for Students about Getting Started in College

Here are some things to consider if you're planning on college studies. If you're like the majority of BHS graduates, you'll begin at a community college. What I say here may be only partially applicable if you'll start at a four-year school.

Of course, you are completely free to go at your studies in a way that makes sense to you; follow my suggestions only if they are fitting.

Which classes should I take?

My answer to this question, and to the ones that follow, is based on the fundamental belief that the most important things as you get started in college are to get settled in, find ways of approaching your classwork that make sense to you and that work for you, enjoy what you're doing, and be successful. For this reason, I recommend that you take whatever classes seem interesting to you. It's safe to do this for at least one term because, unless you take several courses in the same exotic discipline—three courses in advanced cake decorating, for example—it is very hard to "waste" a semester. Anything you might take will count for something down the line: admissions requirements at a four-year school, part of your certificate program or major, breadth requirements, etc. Besides how can you "waste" a semester when you're learning things you want to learn? Even three classes in advanced cake decorating could be rewarding and fulfilling, and might lead to your vocation or an important hobby.

Of course, if you have a clear and certain goal, find out what you need to do to reach it and plan accordingly.

What requirements do I need to meet?

None at all until you decide on a goal. You may want a certificate in vocational gardening or criminal justice, or you may want to earn a two-year degree with a major in history, or you may want to prepare to be admitted as a junior biology major at a four-year university (but don't worry if you don't have such a goal—see above). Until you decide what your goal is, there are no requirements of any kind, except that you follow the general rules of the college and maintain minimum grades.

It's a good idea to have a copy of the college catalog (you can get one online or at the college bookstore) so that you know what the college rules are. And in the catalog you can probably find the requirements that you'll need to meet when you decide on a goal. You'll also probably find, if you do some browsing in the catalog, some goals that you didn't know existed. You can, of course, talk to a counselor at the college.

How many classes should I take?

I don't know. But you may want to consider these questions: Do you want to accomplish something academically in a given period of time? How hard to you want to work during the school term? Will you need time for other things, like a job?

Some of my students have gotten off to a good start in college with one class; others have taken six or seven (don't do this unless you're very devoted to your schoolwork). If going to school will be your main focus, and if you want to be more or less a full-time student, you might want to consider taking three, four, or five classes. If you can't come to a firm decision, sign up for more rather than fewer. You can take a very good look at the workload in each class during the early days of the term and, if you've overloaded yourself, you can drop a class or two (be sure you take care of the paperwork before the deadline, found in the schedule of classes). It's much easier to drop classes than to add them because many are filled by the time classes begin. You are completely free to drop any classes you want; this isn't high school, and there aren't confining rules telling you how to live your life.

What if I don't know what I want to study?

No problem. While some people find their calling early in their lives, many others begin college knowing that they want formal education but not knowing what they want to focus on. One student I worked with attended a community college for three years (rather than two, because she needed to work), transferred to San Jose State University thinking she wanted to be a physical education major, studied with an inspiring chemistry professor, and changed her major. She graduated with great distinction in chemistry and when on to earn a Ph.D. in biochemistry from the University of California, San Francisco. She's now a professor at a college in Massachusetts. Ellen Goodman, a columnist (now retired) who won the Pulitzer Prize, didn't write her first story or know that she would be a journalist until after she graduated from college. My view is that it isn't necessary to always have a specific goal. What matters is being actively engaged in your own life and having some sort of direction; your direction can be very general such as attending college with your eyes wide open to see what you can find there.

A student I worked with, now a university English professor, who became an English major only after she was well into her college studies, wrote, "Time's passage leads to change, and if you are open to these changes, you will undoubtedly grow." If you want to grow into a college major, you will; it's just that you may not be able to predict what inspiration will come your way or when it will arrive. And don't forget Debbie (Chapter 2), who wound up in a doctoral program in high-altitude physiology as a result of watching the movie *Top Gun*.

If you want to keep open the possibility of going on to a four-year college or university, you should plan for this from the beginning. No, I'm not contradicting myself; you can take what you please during your first semester or quarter and pay attention to how your course choices fit into a college admissions scheme. By your second term you will probably want to choose most of your courses according to this scheme. If you do settle on a major early, this will make your planning more straightforward and insure that you spend your time efficiently at your community college (although efficiency isn't necessarily the highest priority).

Will I be OK?

Yes. I have come to believe, based both on my extensive experience and research I've read, that your success will have to do with your optimism, confidence, and sense of independence. Feeling independent is easy when you're in college. You don't have anyone looking over your shoulder telling you not to chew gum, or that you're bad because you're seven seconds late to class, or that you should do your homework each night instead of leave it to do in big chunks (or vice versa). You will be treated as an independent and responsible human being and you'll act accordingly.

Confidence and optimism may be a bit trickier. You may or may not think of yourself as a confident person, but do realize that you've had the courage to resist tons of pressure from our society to go to high school, do all the usual high school stuff, and earn a traditional diploma. And I'm assuming you're somewhat optimistic about college or you wouldn't be going.

You may be scared, but that's not the same thing as lacking confidence. It's possible to be afraid and get on with things anyway. Lots of people who have experienced what you're going to do have been scared, but they've succeeded, and the fear goes away very soon. One of my former students told me that reading Susan Jeffers' book, *Feel the Fear . . . and Do It Anyway*, made a positive difference in her life.

Anything else?

Yes. I've already mentioned the college's schedule of classes and its catalog, but I want to say again that these documents contain important information and you should READ THEM—at least the general rules and policies. In particular, you can wind up with undeserved poor grades on your transcript if you don't know what the rules are. Note the deadlines for dropping (and adding) classes and signing up for different kinds of grading, such as credit/no credit. If you decide not to carry through with a class, do the necessary paperwork and do it before the deadline. If you simply stop going to a class, or wait too long to withdraw, you may end up with an F instead of no grade at all (and no record of your being in the class—if you withdraw early) or a W if you drop later but before the deadline.

There are other important facts, dates, policies, and procedures you need to know about. READ THE RULES!

You can, of course, talk with a college counselor if you need to. Colleges may also have other sources of information such as an office to support transfer students. Each of your instructors will explain class assignments and procedures. Of course you'll read these too, and ask questions if you don't understand.

Take good care of yourself by knowing what the rules are. (Yes, I know, I'm repeating myself, but this is an important message which some students have regretted not following.) And take good care of yourself by finding learning opportunities that nourish your real self

Chapter 4
Writing Transcripts

I write narrative transcripts like the one shown in Chapter 3 for young people who have not completed enough academic work to be eligible for admission to four-year colleges and universities, want to be free of compulsory education, and choose to enter a community college, go to work, travel, or engage in other productive endeavors. These transcripts have, without exception, been accepted at the dozens of community colleges in California where they have been submitted, at community colleges in other states, frequently by employers, and even by one four-year college. A narrative transcript may be acceptable at a community college in your state, and it may also satisfy employers. But a transcript that includes more traditional information like grades, credits, a grade point average, and test scores will be most widely accepted and is essential almost always for direct admission to four-year schools.

Traditional subjects should be included on a more traditional transcript, but they need not be studied in traditional ways. Some colleges have a set of required subjects for admission, and these sets, while often similar, are not always identical. For example, some colleges require two years of high-school-level social science for admission, others require three, and some ask for four. In some cases, specific subjects are required, U.S. History for example. Some colleges recommend a set of preparatory courses, and deviations from this set may be tolerated.

A transcript can show experience gained:

- by completing coursework at community colleges

- through distance learning

- at four-year colleges or universities

- by getting high enough scores on exams like SAT Subject Tests, AP, or CLEP

- in working with tutors or mentors

- at high schools

- by learning entirely on your own

- as a result of being employed

- in doing volunteer work

- by traveling

- through almost any significant life experience

The Rules for Writing Transcripts

There aren't any.

About the Lack of Rules

The format of a high school transcript is not like the structure of a salt crystal or star, determined by a set of physical laws that are a part of the universe. There aren't any natural of cultural laws about what a high school transcript should look like. Don't use a template unless you've thought about the best way to present the abilities, experiences, and accomplishments of the owner of the transcript and decide that a template would work best. What you need to do is produce an original document that's easy to read and understand and as impressive as possible.

In the sections that follow, I'll use words like *courses*, *subjects*, *schoolwork*, and *student* in the broadest sense. For example, any item on a transcript that represents a chunk of learning can be called a course, even if it's something like a camping trip. Prescott College in Arizona provides degrees in Adventure Education, and courses focus on outdoor experience. The University of Connecticut offers courses in puppetry. Reed College in Oregon includes in its curriculum a course titled Retro PE, which includes activities like dodge ball and Capture the Flag. You too can award credit, not only for traditional subjects, but also for *any* activity that has resulted in personal growth and the acquisition of skills and knowledge of any kind.

Overall Organization

This and the following sections may make more sense if you flip back and forth between them and the sample transcripts and transcript entries that begin on page 32.

The top of a transcript should show the name of the school, its address, and other contact and/or identifying information. (Well, yes, there are no rules, but what else would be at the top?) I use my letterhead. Next, the student should be identified. My transcripts give the student's name, address, phone number, date of birth, date of enrollment, and date of graduation. This information is followed by a preamble that briefly describes Beach High School and its philosophy.

The body of the transcript is the record of the student's learning. It's a good idea to record learning in chronological order, at least in sections. This shows progress over time and/or in subject areas. It is also a good idea, for visual appeal if for no other reason, to group courses in some way. Groupings can be according to calendar or traditional school years, or school terms such as semesters or quarters, or according to grade level (9th, 10th, etc.). Groupings can also be according to subject, so that, for example, all English courses are listed together, with some indication of when each course began and ended.

I've written transcripts that vary in length from two pages to 20. If you come to believe that it's best to write a long transcript, I suggest that you put a summary of learning at the beginning in the form of a course list with grades and credits, and then provide details after this summary. You can include a section for "extracurricular" activities if you want to use separate sections for academic coursework and not-so-academic endeavors. I often don't distinguish between the two since I believe that all learning is valuable. For example, I've included "Work Skills" in course lists, an entry showing that a student has held a job.

Course Titles

Course titles should obviously be accurately descriptive, and at least some of the titles should be as traditional-sounding as possible. I believe that, beyond mastery of the three R's, a well-tended curiosity and exposure to a variety of experiences are the central elements in preparation for college. What follows naturally from this belief is that a tour of historic spots of the United States, even if the trip doesn't include a set of places that represents the full sweep of our history, can be honestly listed as U.S. History. You'd be making a mistake if you were to assume that everyone who spent four years in a traditional high school really remembers much of what was presented in classes. Someone who has found some historic sites to be of genuine interest is as well prepared in United States History as most graduates of traditional high schools.

Nontraditional coursework can be included on your transcript along with the traditional courses required for college admission (if college admission is the goal). Several examples of this appear on Suzanna's transcript, courses such as Alternative Education Studies and Australian Culture (see page 33).

It's best to have some descriptive words in course titles so that you don't just list History, but Ancient History, European History, or U.S. History.

It isn't necessary to assign the same amount of credit to all courses, so each course doesn't have to have included the same amount of work. If there's just a little bit of something, include it as part of another course. For example, if a student had spent a lot of time on the culture of Japan and a little on Vietnam and Cambodia, this could presented as one course in Asian Cultures. If the histories of these countries were also studied, even if 80% of the work was on culture and 20% was on history, you could still list that course as Asian Cultures and History. The course description would explain that most attention was paid to Japan, and that the focus was on culture.

If a subject, say English, was studied extensively, you'll want to list several years or semesters of it. Again, be descriptive, so that if the student read a bunch of English novels, list a semester (or more) of The English Novel. You'll also undoubtedly want to include Composition in some or all of your English course titles. Numbers can also be included, as in English 4: Literature, Composition, and Critical Thinking.

You probably won't be able to fit everything perfectly into semesters or quarters (keep in mind, you can include summer sessions or summer quarters). Just make the best approximation you can. For example, if the student studied Greek Mythology from July of 2012 to November of that year, that fits best into the Fall Semester, 2012. (The second semester of the academic year would be the Spring Semester, 2013.) Traditional school years typically begin in August or September and run until the following May or June.

If you list courses by subject instead of in time periods, you can give beginning and ending dates for each course (see Laura's course descriptions on page 40).

Amount of Detail

The amount of detail you include depends on how much evaluative material you have from recognized sources outside your homeschool. If almost everything on the transcript was done at home without outside evaluation, you should include a lot of detail. You can explain how studies were organized, what materials were used, and what activities, such as field trips and lab work, accompanied book work. I most often use course descriptions to provide detail. More detail can be shown in reading lists, descriptive and evaluative letters and statements, names of tutors and mentors and descriptions of their qualifications—anything of substance that you have.

A list of courses with grades and credits should precede the detailed material you include so that admissions officials can see an overall picture of the student's studies by looking at one, two, or three pages, and then proceed to look at the details. You don't want the people who examine the transcript to have to read 15 or 20 pages before they can grasp the big picture.

If a substantial amount of evaluative material from outside your homeschool is on the transcript, you can be much more relaxed about how you record homeschool work. Outside work can include courses taken at traditional, recognized high schools or colleges, work with tutors whose qualifications can be described, test scores, distance learning at both the high school and college levels, and so on.

Once again, there are no rules. Increasingly, I've felt that I can include on or exclude from a transcript anything I want as long as I make it clear what I'm doing. For example, if a student has done work in a traditional school and gotten both high and low grades, I might list just those courses in which the student earned high grades, or just the courses he values. In one case a student of mine, Anna Hutchinson, who had attended a public high school, had been give an A for the first semester of U.S. History and an F for the second semester. I transcribed the A and left off the F, assigning instead an A for the second semester of U.S. History based on Anna's having scored a 5 on the AP Exam and a 740 on the SAT Subject Test in this subject. Part of the preamble on her transcript reads this way:

> In the course listings below, an (OT) indicates a course completed at Oakland Technical High School in Oakland, California; in connection with these courses, a P indicates a college preparatory course, and an H indicates an honors course. Preparatory courses emphasize discussion and critical analysis. OT (and Laney College) courses are listed selectively. Anna's lower grades at OT reflect her understandably unenthusiastic response to unchallenging work. She has demonstrated her knowledge and abilities in other ways.

Anna spent her senior year at Beach High School. She had a tutor for Ancient Greek and completed one community college course, Government and Politics in the United States. She got course credit for her SAT II math score (SAT II tests are now called SAT Subject Tests). The rest of the courses on her transcript for this year represent volunteer work and employment. Her transcript also included a lengthy list of young adult fiction she had read during her four years of high school. She applied to two universities and was accepted by both of them. She is now a graduate of American University.

Assigning Credits and Grades

In many states' public schools, completion of a one-year high school course yields one credit or unit. The number of credits required for graduation is often 22-24. In California, many schools award 10 credits for each year-long class. Variable credit is sometimes possible.

I have really mixed feelings about credits and grades. I think kids' accomplishments are among the most important things in the world, and I also think that any attempt to measure them with numbers and letters has got to be close to meaningless. Anna's very high test scores in U.S. History clearly show that the F on her school record did not reflect what she had learned.

I've read single pages, sentences even, that have changed my life in significant ways, and my encounters with these brief passages have been more important than many classes I've taken. I've talked with students who felt that a trip to Europe or Asia was worth more than four years in high school, and I have no reason to challenge this valuation. How important a learning experience is depends on many things beyond time and effort expended.

I also believe that being propelled by positive emotion—feeling self-confidence, determination, and a sense of autonomy—are more foundational than academic background in the ingredients for contentment and success, even academic success. Many of my students skip big chunks of high school and go on to be very successful in college and in vocational endeavors. There seems to be no correlation between how much course credit they earn in high school and how well they do in college.

So I assign credit based on lots of factors. I ask kids how they value their experiences. I sometimes ask them to compare their life experiences with high school coursework. I also consider the end result, knowing that everything should add up to something close to 230, although one of my students who went to Stanford had a total of 582.3 credits on his transcript. Even when I agree with a kid that some life-changing experience might be worth 500 credits compared with her study of, say, world history, I don't write it down because it would be seen as unreasonable. The highest number of credits I've ever assigned to a course is 75. Suzanna's transcript (on pages 32-37) shows course credit ranging from 3 to 40. I see this whole process as just a game, and I play with it.

Grade Point Average

If you assign grades, you'll probably want to compute a grade point average (GPA) and report both it and the total number of credits. Each credit of A work gets 4 points, each credit of B work gets 3 points, and so on. For a plus, add 0.3 grade point; for a minus, subtract 0.3. You also have the option of assigning an extra grade point for every honors course: an honors course can be one taken in college, an Advanced Placement (AP) or similar course, or one that has demanded an extra effort from the student. You get to decide, but be realistic.

Here's a brief example of computing a GPA using the California scheme for credits:

Course 1	A	8 credits	32 grade points	(4 x 8)
Course 2	B	10 credits	30 grade points	(3 x 10)
Course 3	A-	5 credits	18.5 grade points	(3.7 x 5)
Course 4 (honors)	A	5 credits	25 grade points	(5 x 5)
Total credits:		28		
Total grade points:			105.5	

GPA = grade points divided by credits, rounded to two places: 105.5 / 28 = 3.77

Here's a computation where 1 credit is assigned to a year-long course:

Course 1	A	0.8 credit	3.2 grade points	(4 x 0.8)
Course 2	B	1.0 credit	3 grade points	(3 x 1)
Course 3	A-	0.5 credit	1.85 grade points	(3.7 x 0.5)
Course 4 (honors)	A	0.5 credit	2.5 grade points	(5 x 0.5)
Total credits:		2.8		
Total grade points:			10.55	

GPA = grade points divided by credits, rounded to two places: 10.55 / 2.8 = 3.77

Adding a grade point for honors courses produces a weighted GPA. Since writing Suzanna's and Charlie's transcripts, I've begun reporting both a weighted and an unweighted GPA, since some colleges don't pay attention to a weighted one. In computing an unweighted GPA, treat the grades in honors courses like all other grades.

Class Rank

As in every other part of the transcript, you can make choices about how to deal with class rank, something many colleges will expect to see and will often ask for on application forms. I've seen a homeschool transcript, one which accompanied a successful application to Brown University, that showed a rank of "1 out of 1." It's also perfectly fine to simply say that you don't provide a class rank.

I sometimes provide the statement below with a transcript (on a separate sheet of paper, perhaps along with other explanatory material); I also write this statement on application forms. Many evaluative forms that accompany college applications also ask for the relative difficulty of a student's program:

A Note on Class Ranking and Course Selection at Beach High School

The work for which I grant credit may include independent learning at home; work with mentors in the community; special programs sponsored by schools or other organizations; high school courses taken in public, private, and distance learning schools; community college and university coursework; volunteer work; travel; and training programs and employment. One student may have been aiming for medical school while another learned how to frame houses. Because of the extremely wide variety in my students' programs, I do not rank students, and I also cannot provide a reasonable comparative estimate of how demanding a student's program has been.

Test Scores

Test scores (SAT, ACT, etc.) are a typical component of transcripts, but aren't always necessary. I usually place test scores as they are placed on Suzanna's and Charlie's transcripts (starting on page 32). If the student has passed other tests, perhaps the GED or an exit exam, make a note of this.

I sometimes give course credit for test scores (see course description on page 40). The University of California gives course credit for test scores, and I use their criteria. You can find them by searching the internet for "UC a-g options."

Signatures

Signatures of the people responsible for the homeschool should appear at the end of the transcript. You can be the director, principal, head teacher, a counselor, etc. Choose whatever title sounds good to you.

Seal

If you have an artistic bent, you can devise a seal, but you don't need one; a signature will suffice. For the sake of completeness, I'm showing Beach High School's seal here. It's a rubber stamp; I don't have an embossing tool. I also have this in a gold, embossed, stick-on form for diplomas, but you don't need this either. (The Latin translates, "To be, rather than to seem.")

Sample Transcripts

On the following pages you'll find a partial transcript, an entire transcript, and excerpts from transcripts. All are included here with students' permission. All addresses, phone numbers, and parents' names have been changed; "Suzanna" and the names of teachers at The Stevenson School are fictitious. Suzanna's and Charlie's transcript are not their final ones; they are the ones that accompanied their college applications, submitted during the winter of their last pre-college year.

As her transcript (beginning on page 32) indicates, Suzanna attended a private high school for a year before taking her education into her own hands. Since there were narrative comments on her transcript from this school, I included some excerpts on her BHS transcript which followed the use-what-you-have principle. Suzanna studied the traditional subjects required by the schools she applied to, and she also completed some nontraditional studies, including extensive travel. She applied to California State University, Sacramento and to the University of Washington. She was accepted by both schools and chose to enroll at Sacramento State. At the end of the 2014-2015 academic year, she will be close to graduation. She is focusing on business, wanting to bring the principles of positive psychology into whatever vocation she chooses.

Charlie Smith's full transcript follows Suzanna's partial one. His is an example of a transcript that requires no details because the majority of his work was at a recognized institution, a community college. I felt no need to describe the qualifications of his tutors, something I would have done if he had completed most of his work independently at home.

Charlie applied for early admission to the Tisch School of the Arts at New York University; he learned in December of 2000 that he had been accepted. NYU never asked for a final transcript and I never wrote a final version.

Charlie is a graduate of NYU and has studied at the University of Turin in Italy. He is now (August 2014) managing partner at Charlie Smith Design Associates in New York City, a theatrical and entertainment design firm.

TRANSCRIPT

**Beach
High
School**

3635 Sevilla Drive
Soquel, CA 95073
831-462-5867 • beachhi@cruzio.com

Name: Suzanna Amy Hanson
Address: 1417 Blackberry Lane
Boulderville, CA 37095
Phone: 989-767-5454
Birth Date: 7/23/94
Parents: Warren & Rebecca Hanson
Entered: 8/11/11
Expected graduation date: 5/30/12

Beach High School exists to support students who are gaining an education outside of a traditional high school setting. Suzanna has completed the challenging coursework listed here in a wide variety of enriching ways.

The following symbols are used in the course list below.

ARA – course completed at Athénée Royal Arlon in Arlon, Belgium
SacSt – course completed at Sacramento State University
VE – course completed at Visions in Education, San Juan Unified School District, Carmichael, California
Ind – independent learning
TS – course credit for test scores according to University of California guidelines

Credits earned at the Stevenson School have been converted from 3 per year-long course to 10 per year-long course. Numerical grades from Athénée Royal Arlon have been converted according to the scheme at http://www.wes.org/gradeconversionguide/index.asp, and courses have been assigned credit on a 10 per year-long course basis. College semester units have been multiplied by 3.3 in converting them to high school credits. An (H) denotes an honors course. An asterisk in the grade column indicates a course in progress. Comments by teachers at the Stevenson School, course descriptions, and a reading list follow this course list.

2008-2009 at the Stevenson School in Pebble Beach, California

Course	Grade/Credit	
English 1	A	10.0
World History 1	A	10.0
Latin 1	A	10.0
Algebra 1	A	10.0
Earth & Environmental Science	A	10.0
Introductory Art Studio	A	10.0
Information Technology Literacy	A	3.0
Public Speaking	A	3.0
Physical Education	P	10.0

2009-2010

EDS 99: Special Problems (H)(SacSt)	CR	6.6
HRS 10: Arts and Ideas of the West: Ancient to Medieval (H)(SacSt)	A-	10.0
PE 2 (VE)	A	5.0

2009-2010 (continued)

Biology (VE)	A	5.0
Dir Proj (VE)	A	5.0
Latin 2 (VE)	A	5.0
Honors English 2 (VE)	A	5.0
Australian Culture (Ind)	A	10.0
English: Novel Composition (Ind)	A	10.0
Asian Culture (Ind)	A+	13.0
World History 2 (Ind)	A	10.0
Geometry (Ind)	A	10.0
English: Composition and Literature (TS)	A+	40.0
Intermediate Art (Ind)	A	10.0

2010-2011

Ethics (ARA)	A	7.0
Biology (ARA)	A-	7.0
Social Sciences (ARA)	C	7.0
Art (ARA)	A	7.0
Computer Graphics (ARA)	A	3.0
Belgian and French Cultural and Linguistic Immersion (H)(Ind)	A+	20.0
International Youth Travel Advocacy (Ind)	A	10.0

2011-2012

FREN 2B: Intermediate French (H)(SacSt)	*	13.2
PSYC 2: Introductory Psychology (H)(SacSt)	*	10.0
ALS 57D: Academic Strategies (H)(SacSt)	*	3.3
EDS 99: Special Problems (H)(SacSt)	*	6.6
Psychology and Philosophy (Ind)	*	10.0
Alternative Education Studies (Ind)	*	10.0
Algebra 2 (Ind)	*	10.0
Chemistry (Ind)	*	10.0
Advanced Art (Ind)	*	10.0
U.S. History (Ind)	*	10.0
English: American Literature (Ind)	*	10.0

TOTAL CREDITS COMPLETED: 281.6 (as of 12/15/11)

OVERALL GRADE POINT AVERAGE: 4.18 (as of 12/15/11)

An extra grade point has been added for honors/college courses.

TEST SCORES

SAT

June 5, 2010

Reading 630

Math 540

Writing 720

Comments by teachers at the Stevenson School

Nancy Tensoro wrote: "Suzanna continues to impress. She earned the highest score of all my freshmen on the final [in World History 1], and with some stiff competition. Further, she seems to have improved her effort over these last few weeks and all of her final projects, including a group presentation and a wonderful final world map, were truly her best work. She showed me a renewed commitment not just to earning a grade, but to learning about a new subject and giving her best effort in her studies. I hope as Suzanna moves through school she remembers the point of giving her best even when some of the work comes easy for her. She is a gifted young woman, and while I know her passions lie in other fields, she is a critical thinker and keen analyst as she shows in her history work. I hope she continues to sharpen these skills too."

Amanda Smithson wrote: "Suzanna was a consistently strong student throughout the year of Earth and Environmental Science. She never faltered in her efforts on tests, homework and labs, and she earned an impressive 93.6% test average for the term. Suzanna's commitment to work to her potential, shown in the thoroughness of her homework and the depth in her labs, is very respectable. Suzanna came alive at the end of the term during her PowerPoint presentation on overpopulation and water use. During her research, Suzanna avoided the temptation to oversimplify and her classmates gained insights into the complexities surrounding population growth from her presentation. I have enjoyed Suzanna's amiable nature and her eagerness to learn this year."

Michelle Gerson wrote: "Suzanna has been a delightful young lady to teach and an inspiration to us all. She has exhibited undying curiosity and passion in all projects. She has remarkable talent in art. Her collage and illustrations are a testament to her high level of artistic ability and to her exceptional creativity. I look forward to her continued virtuosity and development in art in the years ahead."

Course descriptions—independent learning

Suzanna's transcript included course descriptions for all her independent-learning courses. Only a few are included here as examples.

Australian Culture

It's hard to imagine a better way to study Australian culture than by traveling down the Gold Coast for seven weeks with just a backpack and a notebook at the ready. Through the avant-garde company Unschool Adventures, home stays were organized from Brisbane to Canberra, from a self-sustaining rainforest farm in Woolgoolga to a week with Australian teens in the outback. Our small group was immersed in Australian culture as we became friends with our hosts, got a private tour of Australia's longest-running jail, Maitland Gaol, catered a wedding, and traveled from Queensland to Victoria through New South Wales. Themes emerged through observation and discussion. I focused on the cost of importation on variety and the practical Australian ethic on lifestyle and architecture. My final project, a dictionary of Australian terms that explored the expression of culture through language, was published on the Unschool Adventures' site.

Alternative Education Studies

This course takes its root in 8th grade but culminates this year as I accomplish this chapter of the experiment and journey that is exploring autodidacticism, or unschooling. It has led me through the history of education and given me the perspective that compulsory education is the experiment. It has been my most challenging course to date in terms of separating its meaning as a study, as my education, and as a representation to others, not only of its viability, but of its advantages. Indeed, this forward thinking has enabled me receive the education that I have. *College Without High School* by Blake Boles and *The Teenage Liberation Handbook* by Grace Llewellyn were the keystone works that opened up this field to me. I now explore themes of the internet's rising role in education, a greater utilization of the community by youth, relevancy of curriculum, and the role of learning being ultimately and innately in the hands of the learner. As I continue, I will be using Peter Gray's blog "Freedom to Learn," various TED education videos, Ken Robinson's RSA Animates, and Grace Llewellyn's Not Back To School Camp as resources in addressing critique. I plan to expose my conclusions online, follow the news in education, and study Maria Montessori, John Holt, and John Taylor Gatto.

U.S. History

An overview of American History from 1775-present initiates this course and gives a timeline with which to compare figures and events. Presidents and important events are memorized and summaries are written. The primary text is *The Americans* by Gerald A. Danzer, J. Jorge Klor De Alva, and Larry S. Krieger. Supplementary resources will be used to expand upon concepts. A trip to Washington D.C. and the visitation of its monuments and museums will put U.S. History into modern-day perspective.

English: American Literature

Senior year English complements the study of U.S. History by featuring works of American literature to gain an in-depth view of the years in which the books are written or take place. Items on the reading list are *Walden* by Henry Thoreau, *Leaves of Grass* by Walt Whitman, *The Great Gatsby* by F. Scott Fitzgerald, *The Scarlet Letter* by Nathaniel Hawthorne, and many more. Selections from *An Anthology of Famous American Stories* by Angus Burrell and Bennett Cerf include such classic authors as Mark Twain, Washington Irving, Edgar Allen Poe, O. Henry, and Ernest Hemingway. A cumulative project with a composition and extensive reading will be completed on author(s) of choice.

Reading List

These works, largely chosen independent of any directed curriculum, excluding textbooks, and often encountered by chance, have influenced new interests, especially those indicated with an asterisk, and in that way may be an example of the path that I have taken. I regret that while this list is to the best of my memory, it is not comprehensive, and cannot encompass the range of written and unwritten works from which I have benefitted. The dagger symbol indicates I am currently reading the book.

Early Reading

Grimm's Complete Fairytales by the Brothers Grimm, **Alice in Wonderland** by Lewis Carroll, **Through the Looking-Glass** by Lewis Carroll, **The BFG*** by Roald Dahl, The **Harry Potter** Series* by J.K. Rowling, **The True Confessions of Charlotte Doyle** by Avi, **Jane Eyre*** by Charlotte Brontë, **To Kill a Mockingbird** by Harper Lee, **Of Mice and Men** by John Steinbeck, **Cannery Row** by John Steinbeck, **Anne Frank** by Anne Frank, **The Giver*** by Lois Lowry, **Gathering Blue** by Lois Lowry, **Nonsense Novels** by Stephen Leacock, **Kingston By Starlight** by Christopher John Farley, **A Portrait of the Artist As a Young Man** by James Joyce, **The Prince†** by Niccolo Machiavelli, **Sadako and the Thousand Paper Cranes** by Eleanor Coerr and Ronald Himler

Subscribed to **Psychology Today** to present.

Freshman Year

The Odyssey* by Homer, **The Catcher in the Rye*** by J.D. Salinger, **The Tempest** by Shakespeare, **The Epic of Gilgamesh**, **Big Fish** by Daniel Wallace, **The Lord of the Flies** by William Golding, **The Book Without Words** by Avi, **A Separate Peace** by John Knowles, **The Secret Life of Bees** by Sue Monk Kidd, **Into the Wild** by Jon Krakauer

Sophomore Year

Oedipus Rex by Sophocles, **Antigone** by Sophocles, **Tristan and Iseult**, **The Inferno*** by Dante, **Your First Novel*** by Ann Rittenburg, **No Plot? No Problem!** by Chris Baty, **Characters, Emotion, and Viewpoint** by Nancy Kress, **Snoop** by Sam Gosling, **Banquet of the Damned** by Adam Nevill, **The Nature of Monsters** by Clare Clark, **The Teenage Liberation Handbook*** by Grace Llewellyn, **The New Global Student*** by Maya Frost, **Life of Pi** by Yann Martel, **Bel Canto*** by Ann Patchett, **Emotional Intelligence*** by Daniel Goleman, **The Republic*†** by Plato, **Tao Te Ching*** by Lao Tzu, translation by Stephen Mitchell, **The Tao of Pooh** by Benjamin Hoff, **The Tao of Daily Life** by Derek Lin, **The Blood of Flowers** by Anita Amirrezvani, **Men Are From Mars, Women are from Venus** by John Gray, PhD, **One Hundred Years of Solitude†** by Gabriel García Márquez

Junior Year

The Republic of Trees by Sam Taylor, **Third Culture Kids** by David C. Pollock and Ruth Van Reken

In French: **L'Interprétation des Rêves (The Interpretation of Dreams)** (Chapter 1) by Sigmund Freud, **La Reveuse d'Ostende (The Woman with the Bouquet)** by Eric- Emmanuel Schmitt, **Le Monde de Sophie* (Sophie's World)** by Jostein Gaarder, **La Nausée* (The Nausea)** by Jean-Paul Sartre.

Senior Year (as of 10/27/11)

Stumbling on Happiness* by Daniel Gilbert, **Opportunities After 'High School'** by Wes Beach, **You Majored in What?** by Katharine Brooks, **Walden*†** by Thoreau, **The Price of Everything†** by Russell Roberts, **Who's Your City?** by Richard Florida, **An Incomplete Education†** by Judy Jones and William Wilson, **The Honor Code: How Moral Revolutions Happen†** by Kwame Anthony Appiah, **Guns, Germs, and Steel†** by Jared M. Diamond, **An Anthology of Famous American Stories†** by Angus Burrell and Bennett Cerf.

A Sample of Educational Films and Documentaries

> **One Flew Over the Cuckoo's Nest**
> **Pride and Prejudice**
> **Romeo and Juliet**
> **The Sound of Music**
> **Doctor Zhivago**
> **Gone with the Wind**
> **Bienvenue Chez les Ch'tis**
> **The Greatest Movie Ever Sold (Product Placement Documentary)**
> **True Grit**
> **John Adams (HBO Documentary)**
> **Anna Karenina**
> **Schindler's List**
> **The Help**
> **Brain Games (National Geographic)**

Signed:_____

Wes Beach, Director

Seal:

Date:_____

TRANSCRIPT

Name: Charles R. Smith
Address: 4321 Greenbrae Ave.
Blue Hill, CA 37059
Phone: 138-555-4123
Birth Date: 12/29/83
Parents: Carl & Martha Smith
Entered: 6/4/98
Graduated: —

Beach
High
School

3635 Sevilla Drive
Soquel, CA 95073
831-462-5867 • beachhi@cruzio.com

Charlie's records from Georgiana Bruce Kirby Preparatory School show the following work completed. Course credit has been converted from 4 units/year to 10 credits/year.

1997-98 school year			**1997-98 school year (continued)**		
Course	Grade/Credit		Course	Grade/Credit	
Geometry	B	10.0	Art 2A	P	5.0
Physics	C-	10.0	Theater Prod.: Set Design	A	5.0
Eng 9: Medieval Literature	B-	10.0	Play Production	P	5.0
Hist 9: Middle Ages	B-	10.0	Physical Education	P	5.0
French II	B	10.0			

Beach High School exists to support students who want to gain an education outside of a traditional high school setting. We have supported Charlie in completing the following coursework with the institutions listed.

Unmarked coursework was at Cabrillo College in Aptos, California.
(IU) indicates a course through correspondence with Indiana University.
(KE) indicates a course through correspondence with Keystone National High School.
(SC) indicated a course through correspondence with the University of Southern Colorado.
(T) indicates a course completed with a tutor.
College semester units have been multiplied by 3.3 to convert to high school credits.

Summer 1997	**Grade/Credit**	
French 1–Beginning	A	13.2
Fall 1998		
Art 2A–Drawing and Composition	A	10.0
Art 50L–Gallery Viewing Lab	CR	1.7
Theatre Arts 27–Theatre Production Workshop	A	6.6
English 10 (T)	A	5.0
French 3 (T)	B	5.0
Algebra 2 (T)	A	5.0
Spring 1999		
Theatre Arts 31–Intro to Design in the Theatre	A	10.0
History 4B–Survey of Western Civilization	C	10.0
Biology (KE)	A	10.0
English 10 (T)	A	5.0

Spring 1999 (continued)

French 3 (T)	B	5.0
Algebra 2 (T)	A	5.0

Fall 1999

Art 4–Beginning Design: Design and Color	A	10.0
Theatre Arts 27–Theatre Production Workshop	A	3.3
Theatre Arts 34–Costume Workshop	B	10.0
French 3–Intermediate	C	13.2
History 201–United States to 1877 (SC)	B	10.0
Pre-Calculus (T)	A	5.0

Spring 2000

Theatre Arts 27–Theatre Production Workshop	A	3.3
History 17B–United States History Since 1865	B	10.0
French 4–Intermediate	C	13.2
Anthro 1–Introduction to Anthropology: Physical	B	13.2
English W131–Elementary Composition 1 (IU)	B+	10.0
Pre-Calculus (T)	A	5.0

Fall 2000

Oceanography 10–Introduction to Oceanography	*	13.2
Theatre Arts 31–Intro to Design in the Theatre	*	10.0
Theatre Arts 27–Theatre Production Workshop	*	3.3
Art 50L–Gallery Viewing Lab	*	1.7
English 1B–Composition and Literature	*	10.0
Math 119–Brief Survey of Calculus I (IU)	*	10.0

*In progress

Spring 2001

English 30A–American Literature	*	10.0
Political Science 1–Introduction to Government	*	10.0
Art 3A–Life Drawing	*	10.0
Math 119 (continued) (IU)	*	

*Planned

OVERALL GRADE POINT AVERAGE THROUGH SPRING 2000: 3.78

TEST SCORES

Exam	Date	Score
SAT I Verbal	Jun00	640
SAT I Math	Jun00	520
SAT II French with Listening	Nov99	600
SAT I Verbal	Jun99	550
SAT I Math	Jun99	550

Seal:

Signed: _____

Wes Beach, Director

Date: _____

Transcript / Charles R. Smith / page 2 of 2

More Course Descriptions

Laura Deming's story is in my book *Forging Paths: Beyond Traditional Schooling*. Here I'll simply say that she never attended any K-12 school, began doing serious research at the University of California, San Francisco at age 12, and was accepted at MIT when she was 14. She spent two years at MIT, won a Thiel Fellowship, and is now (August 2014) a partner in a venture capital firm in San Francisco that supports anti-aging research.

The course descriptions below are from Laura's transcript. Only one of the four courses described below involved attending classes at a school. Algebra and Geometry, for 30 credits (three years' worth), was based on test scores; Calculus with Analytic Geometry was done independently; and Classical Mechanics was based on course materials from MIT.

Algebra and Geometry: The mathematics requirement for freshman admission to the University of California is "[t]hree years of college-preparatory mathematics that include the topics covered in elementary and advanced algebra and two- and three-dimensional geometry." The University considers the entire three-year requirement to be met by a score of 480 or higher on SAT Mathematics Level 2 Subject Exam. Laura's score was 800.

Calculus with Analytic Geometry, 3/07–7/07: After I worked through the Saxon calculus book, I got the textbook MIT uses for their calculus courses, *Calculus with Analytic Geometry* (Simmons) and started working problems from it. These problems were much more complex and required creative thinking; sometimes a problem would take days to solve. It was like a crash course for my calculus skills. I also did part of the MIT textbook for multivariable calculus, *Multivariable Calculus* (Edwards & Penney).

Classical Mechanics 8.01, MIT OpenCourseWare, 3/07–6/07: Taught by the engaging Prof. Lewin, these lectures emphasized the basic concepts of Newtonian mechanics, fluid mechanics, and kinetic gas theory. A variety of other interesting topics were also covered in this course: binary stars, neutron stars, black holes, resonance phenomena, musical instruments, stellar collapse, supernovae, and a peek into the intriguing quantum world. The professor's devotion to the subject (he risked his life in the name of conservation of motion) made this course an unforgettable experience. I watched these lectures and took extensive notes, then decided to take the Berkeley course for credit. Text: *Physics, Volume 1, 3rd Edition,* by Robert Resnick and David Halliday.

Physics X412–Physics-A, UCB, 9/07–12/07: I wanted to get credit for a physics course, so I took this class at Berkeley Extension. This course was like a first-year introductory physics course with an emphasis on mechanics. It covered things like "properties of matter, kinetics, thermodynamics, heat, wave motion, fluids, and sound." Text: *College Physics,* Young & Geller.

Another Kind of Transcript

For the first time ever, during the spring of 2014, I wrote a transcript for a student headed to a four-year university that did not include course descriptions. Anna had been entirely homeschooled and had become a highly accomplished musician; the harp is her instrument of choice. Her transcript began with the usual list of courses, grades, and credits, but was followed by four statements in English prose and a list of concerts, events, and musical studies that Anna had participated in which were not in the course list. The four statements were from her father; her harp teacher, a very accomplished and well-known harpist; an English teacher who taught in private settings; and Anna herself. In the fall of 2014 Anna began studies at

Indiana University and its Jacobs School of Music. In an email she sent me a few days before classes started, she wrote, "I'm very excited, more and more so, about all my classes and possibilities over the next four years."

Her father's statement from her transcript follows.

Anna has been homeschooled since before kindergarten. Both her mother and I (her father) have played an active role in all aspects of her education. Her mother concentrated in the early years on reading, writing and basic arithmetic. In those days, my focus was on the explaining how things work in nature, and the various machines surrounding Anna's ever-expanding world. Anna and I could engage in small home experiments and discussions that would foster the basic underpinnings to the scientific method. With time, those questions expanded to museum trips, field trips, home experiments and eventually to more formal curricula using standard textbooks—algebra, geometry, physical science, biology, etc.

Physics and math were also taught outside the strict confines of the textbook pages. Fractions, rates and statistics came up every day in some form or another. Every car trip involved questions on kinematics, while car accidents and safety belts provided fertile ground for lessons on Newtonian dynamics and the principles of Conservation of Momentum and Energy. Plane trips provided opportunities for teaching the basic concepts of lift, drag and Bernoulli's law. The latter principle was reinforced while adjusting the garden hose nozzle while watering the lawn. Wave mechanics were covered at the harp—those strings set up standing waves and harmonics. And tuning covers the basic relation between the frequency and the string's weight, length and tension. Thermodynamics, optics and the laws of electricity were touched on in various activities that included her love of weather and meteorology, rifle shooting and home repairs of lights, fans and wall switches. Chemistry of course was touched on in her cooking chores, as well as discussions of ballistics and modern ammunition. And electrochemistry was introduced while replacing the batteries in one of the many electronic devices around the house. The ubiquitous talk of recycling and waste leads to long discussions about chemicals, chemical stability and polymers. Math lessons were equally reinforced in everyday activities. The world is full of geometric shapes and relationships. Most every news story involves some use—or misuse—of statistics. We found many opportunities to solve for Algebra's missing x, and Calculus is mainly about sums, rates, and changing rates.

Throughout all of these "lessons," Anna proved to be an interested and observant student. Across the topical spectrum she tended to focus more on the principles underneath the phenomena, and less on the operational aspects. Anna is quick to pick up a new concept and less keen on the mechanics and drills for reinforcing the concepts. That will be her strength in the future, because general principles are remembered longer than specific algorithms, and they can be applied to a broader spectrum of future phenomena and problems. I have every confidence that Anna will succeed in any basic math or science course she may choose to take at the college level. More importantly, she has acquired many of the foundational principles and instincts needed to function in an increasingly technological world. This does not necessarily mean that she can repair a hardware or software problem as it arises on her computer. These are specialized tasks that require specific skills and extended exposure to a narrow field. Her science and math education is more general, and can serve as a jumping-off point for future studies if she so chooses.

But Anna has chosen Music as her career choice. That choice was a natural consequence of her exposure at an early age to classical music at home. But it also reflects her desires and talents. Anna has a deep love for music. Her love of music is a necessary prerequisite to succeeding as an adult musician. But she has also been gifted with fine teachers, an excellent ear and exposure to a wide range of musical assignments. Anna has played harp and piano as a soloist, and in small ensembles and many local community orchestras. This has honed her sight reading skills, and given her the opportunity to learn new music on short notice. There is much more to learn, and much more discipline that she will need to become the musician to which she aspires. The Harp Department at Indiana University is a recognized center of excellence, and we have every expectation and hope that the community of musicians there will provide the place for Anna to mature as a musician and capable adult.

Anna has completed studies in all of the topical areas typical of a standard secondary education. These include history, literature, writing and speech, languages, religious studies, mathematics, science, swimming, and the fine arts. It is natural of course, that her love of music has led her to emphasize that area of her studies. I have taught and prepared high-school students in science and mathematics for more than 10 years and am confident that Anna has successfully completed the work necessary to be awarded her diploma and succeed in her future endeavors. Anna herself is ready and motivated to move on to the next phase of her life. It is Anna's motivation and determination to work toward her goals that is the best recommendation for her graduation to the next phase of her education.

When a Transcript May Not Be Required

In some states community colleges have open admission policies, and a homeschool-issued diploma unaccompanied by a transcript may be sufficient for entry. Even this much may not be required. In California, anyone who is 18 years or older is admitted to community college on the basis of age alone. After a solid record has been established at a community college, transfer admission to many (but not all) four-year colleges and universities is based solely on the community college record; no high school documents are necessary.

Chapter 5
Choosing and Applying to Colleges

When to Start College

Laurence Steinberg, in his fascinating book *Age of Opportunity*, defines adolescence as a life period that begins at around age 10 and continues until one's mid-twenties. During this time a person's brain has an especially large capacity for learning complex and important life skills such as self-control and understanding the likely consequences of possible courses of action. Adolescence lasts much longer than it did in the past, and this is a good thing *provided* that you continue to engage in novel and challenging experiences.

Preparing for and attending college can be richly rewarding experiences, but so can other ventures. There's no universally mandated life plan that requires you to go to college (see Chapter 7). If you're college bound, you don't have to focus entirely on academics as you prepare for college and then go to college immediately after you've completed your pre-college studies. You saw in Chapter 3 that, after attending college for a brief period, Torrey spent time traveling and then living and working outside her home state before she returned and continued her college education. Suzanna, whose partial transcript is in Chapter 4, had traveled in more than 25 countries by the time she was 17; she went to college at a typical age. Laura, also in Chapter 4, went to MIT when she was 15, but left after two years to become a partner in a venture capital firm. She may or may not go back to college.

You can go to college, or back to college, at any point in your life. I went directly from high school to UCLA and graduated in 1961; I completed work on a master's degree in 1987 at age 49. My granddaughter Amanda, after a number of unfocused years during her adolescence and early twenties, had a child, got married, moved to Indiana where her parents were, started over at a community college, transferred to the Kelley School of Business at Indiana University, and obtained her bachelor's degree in accounting at age 32. In Chapter 6 you'll read about Cristl Walker's long path to college.

Sometimes going to college early is what works best, as it has for Dalton Hildreth. Here's his story, as told by his mother Jacelyn.

Dalton is a 14-year-old boy who has always been very advanced academically (about six grades ahead), and currently attends the University of Minnesota full-time, majoring in computer science, as approximately a third-year student. Dalton is also a very happy, social child, with many friends his age and activities outside of his classes. As his mom, I have tried very hard to help meet his social and academic needs equally. His social needs have been met very well, but we have not yet been able to meet his academic needs completely.

As a baby, most everything seemed to come quickly and early for Dalton. At about 12 months, he had a vocabulary of over 100 words and spoke in three-word sentences. Around age three he started reading on his own as well as writing short words. At age four, he was adding and subtracting, multiplying and dividing on his own. At age five he was reading third-grade chapter books, and wrote an adventure story with pictures in a small notebook. When he had just turned six he read *Harry Potter* in a week. He was constantly writing stories and drawing detailed diagrams, maps, charts, and coded languages. He needed paper and pencil at all times. He was hungry to learn, in every subject.

Around ages six or seven, he was reading encyclopedias and medical journals we had at home. Around this time we also discovered he had been doing algebra on the back of his school math sheets. We found out he had been watching his older brother (in 10th grade at the time) do his homework. Right when he turned seven, he also started writing a fantasy/adventure novel, complete with drawings of all the characters and fictitious animals, a map of the land, statistical information about their lives, their families, their ships, villages, crops, climate, currency, etc.

In first and second grade, he would come home from school begging for us to give him math/algebra problems to do, then ask non-stop questions wanting to learn more about the things he'd read in his encyclopedias. He would beg his Dad to explain more chemistry and physics to him at night when he'd get home.

Knowledge is like air to Dalton. He is on a relentless quest for knowledge and devours books and information, however he can get it. He grasps concepts very quickly, then will immediately look for ways to apply the knowledge he learns.

Because of all this, at age seven, we pulled Dalton from school and started homeschooling him to try to meet his academic needs. We loved homeschooling, the freedom to learn what, when and how we wanted, as well as all the friends we made with this. We found a homeschool group for highly-gifted children that we met with once a week for fun, challenging, out-of-the-box classes. These became his best friends, and still are to this day!

However, by age 10, we had run out of what we could teach Dalton at home. We were waving the white flag.

So, when he had just turned 11, after much planning, he started part-time at the private high school where his older brother was then a senior. I came with him, and sat nearby in the teacher's lounge while he was in class. He started with pre-calculus and some other classes, but these quickly became painfully easy for him. So, mid-year, we added having him attend the nearby community college part-time, taking computer science classes. This was after about a year of planning to make this happen. However, these ended up being too easy for him as well, and he was also working at a completely different (higher) level than the adults in the classes.

Dalton continued part-time at the high school (taking mostly Advanced Placement classes there) and part-time at the community college for another couple years. Everyone at the high school and community college was very good to him. He made friends there, and joined after-school activities such as math team, science club, chess, and knowledge bowl. He also had instructors at the high school and community college who would talk with him after classes and help mentor him.

However, once again, we had run out of what we could do for Dalton at the high school and community college. Nothing so far, at all, had been a challenge for Dalton. Everything came easy for him, and he had straight A's in everything he did, without really ever studying. He desperately craved a challenge.

So, after working on it for over a year, he started full-time at the university (with mom driving and staying on campus near him). The process took a while, because of problems we ran into due to his age, and the amount of college credits he already had (about 65 at this point). But I just kept making connections, talking to people, and pursuing all his options. He's done very well at the university, finding his way around and making friends in classes (other high-achieving students). He still wishes for a more interesting and stimulating challenge, but it's working for now. I've known for a long time that his challenge will most likely be at the graduate level and through research.

Finding ways to meet Dalton's needs has not always been an easy journey; it has come unchartered and been very overwhelming at times, but to not pursue having his needs met was never an option for me. As overwhelming and crazy as it's been at times, I have cherished the privilege of being Dalton's full-time advocate, advisor, chauffeur, and chaperone—but mostly of just being his mom.

Choosing Colleges to Apply To

In my view, the two most important criteria for choosing colleges to apply to are, first and obviously, whether the colleges have academic programs in the area(s) you're interested in, and second, whether the college campus and community are places where you feel comfortable. Your comfort will depend on your personality and preferences. Do you want to go to college in an urban, suburban, or rural environment? Do you want to be on a campus with tens of thousands of other people, or would you prefer a smaller school? Do you want a considerable amount of flexibility so you can have a hand in designing your own studies? Do you want a college education that includes study abroad or work experience? Do you want to be close to museums, theaters, and other places of enlightenment and entertainment? Do you want to be able to get quickly to a beach, or go skiing on weekends without traveling far, or have nearby places to hike?

You may want to answer some of the questions I've suggested and others before you start learning about colleges, or you may want to start your search first to get a better idea of what questions you're most interested in asking. There are lots of ways to search, and there is no single "right" way. You can talk with family members, friends, neighbors, teachers, counselors, and others about the colleges they attended. You can talk with people you don't know. For example, if you've very interested in, say, psychology, contact people at two- and four-year colleges who teach this subject and ask them where to find strong programs in psychology. You can learn from websites such as collegeconfidential.com. You can attend college fairs. You can read guidebooks such as the latest edition of *Fiske Guide to Colleges*. A good way to get an idea of the wide range of colleges and their programs is to take a look at the book *Cool Colleges for the Hyper-Intelligent, Self-Directed, Late Blooming, and Just Plain Different*. You can study colleges' websites and read their literature and catalogs. Take with a grain of salt what you read and hear in colleges' promotional literature and official tours; each college will want to tell you how great it is. You can certainly conduct a college search on your own, but you can also hire a private counselor.

The single best way to judge your comfort on a college campus is to visit it if you possibly can. Talk to students on the campus and in the student center, sit in on classes (after getting each professor's or instructor's permission), go into dorms and talk with people there, take your own as well as an official tour of the campus, sit under a tree and soak up the feeling of the campus, and make appointments to talk with professors in subjects you might major in.

In your college search, you will have found information about what each college looks for and how selective it is. As you compile the list of colleges you'll apply to, a list that should include several schools, make sure there are a couple colleges where your studies, GPA, and test scores give you a very good chance of being admitted. And don't hesitate to apply to a couple schools where you think your chances are minimal.

There is near hysteria in our country at present about getting into places like Harvard, Yale, and Stanford. There is no guarantee that any one of the very selective schools is the best place for you. Many hundreds of colleges and universities offer a very solid education, and your focus should be on finding a good fit, not on joining the rat race to get into the most prestigious school.

One of my former students earned her bachelor's degree at Troy State University in Dothan, Alabama, and her master's at the University of Minnesota Duluth; these are two schools you've probably never heard of (the flagship campus of the University of Minnesota is in Minneapolis). This graduate of BHS is now happily engaged in teaching mathematics at a community college near Chicago. Another of my former students is, as I write this, very contented in finishing up his undergraduate education at Stanford. Both of these people found a good fit, which, as I've said, is the important thing.

Obtaining Information

During the time you're choosing colleges to apply to, and after you've settled on some choices, you'll want to have a good sense of what the colleges are like and how they operate. There are no general answers to many questions such as, *What subjects do I need to have studied to be eligible for college admission?* Although the set of required preparatory subjects is similar at many schools, it can vary considerably. Taking math as an example, you may be required to have taken two years of this subject to be eligible for admission at Rainbow University, but the University of Technology requires four years.

You'll want to look carefully at each college or university you may apply to. To obtain accurate information, get it from as close to the source as you can. The best source of information about Rainbow University is Rainbow University. Still, incomplete, confusing, and inaccurate information about schools can come from the schools themselves. For example, I once worked briefly with a young man who had a shot at getting an athletic scholarship from a public university in the Midwest. I looked at this school's website and read that all applicants, both freshman and transfer, were required to have a high school diploma. Knowing that this is not true at many schools, I called the admissions office at this college. Here's how the conversation went. "I read on your website that all applicants must have a high school diploma. Will you accept a GED Certificate in lieu of a traditional diploma?" "Yes, we will." "Is a transfer applicant with some minimum number of units required to have a high school diploma?" "No, anyone with 30 or more college semester units need not have a high school diploma." So much for everyone needing a high school diploma.

A transfer applicant is a person who has completed college work before she applies to a school. Many colleges and universities have a transfer admission requirement that makes applicants who have earned minimum number of transferable college units, typically 24 or 30 semester units, eligible for admission solely on the basis of their college records. There may or may not be subject requirements, and standardized test scores may or may not be required.

Questions about freshman versus transfer admission and many other issues have varying answers at different schools: How is the distinction made between freshman and transfer applicants? Is a high school diploma required? If so, must it come from an accredited school? Are standardized test scores required? How is previous college work credited? Is credit for scores on AP and CLEP exams granted, and if so, how?

Admission information can best be obtained by reading material from each college of interest and by communicating with people in admissions offices. To get accurate answers to questions you may have, *it's important to ask carefully crafted questions*. Contact admissions offices as often as you need to. You may need to talk more than one person and ask your questions in as many ways as you can. Record the names of the people you talk with and the dates of conversations. If a person you talk to says things like "I think" or "That's probably so" or gives other signs of not really knowing, ask politely to talk to someone who can give you a definitive answer.

Applying to Colleges

Many colleges accept the Common Application, and you'll be required to set up an account at www.commonapp.org, create an application, and arrange for others to send in documents, including the School Report (more about this later). Some schools require their own supplement to the Common App. Other colleges have their own application forms and procedures. Be sure to carefully study all the appropriate websites so that you know what you need to prepare and the deadlines for submission. It's a good idea to make a master timeline or calendar for yourself so that you can allow plenty of time to carefully complete forms and write thoughtful essays, and so that you won't miss deadlines.

You will most likely be required to write one or more essays as part(s) of your college applications. For the 2014-2015 application season, the Common Application provides five choices as topics for an essay of a maximum of 650 words. Here are two of them:

- Some students have a background or story that is so central to their identity that they believe their application would be incomplete without it. If this sounds like you, then please share your story.

- Discuss an accomplishment or event, formal or informal, that marked your transition from childhood to adulthood within your culture, community, or family.

In writing essays and in completing all other parts of college application, *be yourself;* your college applications should say, in effect, *This is the real me.* Each college is a real place, and you are a real person. The object of the game is to find a real fit, and you won't succeed if you present an invented self that you think admissions committees will like. Your application materials will have far more power if their contents come from your authentic self. If a college doesn't like who you are, why would you want to go there?

In your essays you should present new information, not summarize or even include what the rest of your application says to admission committees. For example, the Report asks you to attach your transcript; it lists coursework, and it would be redundant and a waste of valuable space to describe coursework that you've completed. On the other hand, if you had especially rich and meaningful experiences in learning, say, history, you can go beyond the course description that's on your transcript and describe these experiences and what they have meant to you. In general, your essay should cover what the rest of the application does not say. It should include a lot of specific, detailed information and also paint a full and attractive picture of at least some significant part of your character, accomplishments, interests, and/or potential.

As I write this, Suzanna (whose transcript is in Chapter 4) is close to graduating from California State University, Sacramento. Here is her advice about applying to colleges.

> Your educational priorities and individual skills are the most important parts of the college selection and application process. Don't be daunted by schools. Show your enthusiasm for and commitment to learning—it is more powerful than grades, and wise educators know that. When applying, talk to as many people as you can, and look for answers to your questions from multiple people—you'll get different answers. (Wes taught me that.) The lines of college acceptance are not hard and fast. I hear repeatedly, "Do not play down your uniqueness." Take all the experiences which have most prepared you, pull a theme from them, and promote that in your applications. Whereas a traditional view might be to downplay the semester your grades dropped because you took up archery, Urdu, or underwater basket weaving, I recommend addressing this specifically and explaining how it helped you get where you are today.

> Unlike standardization suggests, you are not a set of checked or unchecked boxes. Academic success roots in personal success; therefore, your life accomplishments and skills recommend your potential. Skills like resilience, curiosity, motivation, and creativity, among many others, are instrumental to people of all disciplines and careers.

There is a substantial amount of scientific evidence to back up what Suzanna says; a lot of it is in Laurence Steinberg's book, mentioned at the beginning of this chapter. Steinberg, a professor of psychology at Temple University, convincingly argues that self-control, motivation, self-confidence, and an ability to work hard, persevere, and look toward the future are very important in success in college and in life.

Whether an interview is required or an option you choose, learn as much as you practically can about the college beforehand so you can answer and ask questions in a knowledgeable way. As in the essay, be yourself.

The School Report

The Common Application process requires a School Report and later, follow-up reports. Schools that do not accept the Common App may have similar forms. These reports ask for things like GPA, rank in class, and checked boxes and a narrative relating to evaluation, along with facts about the school such as the size of its graduating class and the racial and ethnic makeup of its student body. The application that's associated with the Common App must be submitted online, but, in 2014, it's still possible for a school to submit the School Report on paper, a choice I make because it provides more flexibility. Somewhere in the application and/or supporting documents you'll be able to say that you're a homeschooler, so reporting a class rank of 1 and a class size of 1 (or maybe 2 or more if you have siblings) will not seem strange to admission officials.

When I prepare a School Report, I write asterisks in spaces that call for a student's class rank, the size of my graduating class, and AP and IB course offerings; in nearby spaces I write "See attached note." As I previously discussed in Chapter 4, the note is written on a separate sheet of paper and says:

A Note on Class Ranking and Course Selection at Beach High School

The work for which I grant credit may include independent learning at home; work with mentors in the community; special programs sponsored by schools or other organizations; high school courses taken in public, private, and distance learning schools; community college and university coursework; volunteer work; travel; and training programs and employment. One student may have been aiming for medical school while another learned how to frame houses. Because of the extremely wide variety in my students' programs, I do not rank students, and I also cannot provide a reasonable comparative estimate of how demanding a student's program has been.

Students graduate from Beach High School on a rolling basis, and there is no graduating class in the usual sense.

Access to AP, IB, and honors courses varies from student to student, so it is not possible to report the number of such classes at BHS.

A narrative evaluation is part of the School Report. The 2014 Common App says simply, "Please provide comments that will help us differentiate this student from others." A parent or other homeschool "staff" person can certainly write this. You can also ask someone who knows you and whose qualifications might be more readily recognized by the colleges. This person can be a community college instructor, a high school teacher, a tutor with a degree in his field, or anyone else with the credentials or degrees usually held by people preparing traditional students for college. I'm not saying that your homeschool "staff" are not completely capable, simply that outside educators are the people colleges normally rely on.

Whoever writes the evaluation, she (or he) should mention her working relationship with you and any degrees held and/or other qualifications. As I said above in connection with your essay, this narrative should present mostly new material, not just repeat what's in other parts of the application.

Here's what I wrote on Charlie Smith's School Report. His transcript (in Chapter 4) clearly shows that he is academically able. Charlie knew for certain that he wanted his studies to be in theater arts, and an interview with NYU people had gone very well. I felt that it was appropriate for my written piece to focus mostly on the development of Charlie's interest in drama and specifically set design.

For Charlie Smith, the theater is not an interest, or a college major, or even a passion. It's a calling.

When Charlie was three, he built a train in his yard out of cardboard boxes and a variety of materials, a train with bells and whistles. His passion for trains lasted until he discovered the Civil War and became enamored with images of this time in history. In elementary school he organized two second grade classes to create a Civil War reenactment. When he was nine the film *Jurassic Park* claimed his imagination. He built dinosaurs out of foam rubber and aluminum, using discarded auto seat motors to construct moving mouths. He put up a dinosaur display in his front yard – everything went in the *front* yard. His knowledge led to his becoming a docent at the

Santa Cruz Natural History Museum, where he became known as "The Professor." In another setting he wound up—at age ten—instructing high school students.

At Thanksgiving of 1994 Charlie saw *The Phantom of the Opera*. His parents had to pry his fingers loose from the back of a seat to get him to leave the theater. It was at this point that they realized that Charlie hadn't had serial obsessions with trains, the Civil War, and dinosaurs, but that he had a wonderful imagination and a talent for turning images in his head into replicas of reality. The trains, the staging of the Civil War, and the dinosaurs were all aspects of his increasing skill with stagecraft.

Charlie now has a substantial amount of college work in theater to his credit, and he has been hired by Cabrillo Stage, where his salary was recently doubled in recognition of his talent. He is assisting in teaching a high school stagecraft class. And his imagination and ingenuity continue to grow. For the 1999 production of *Playboy of the Western World* at Cabrillo College, he spent three weeks developing a hot coal that could be dropped on an actor without causing injury. He solved the problem with high-density foam, a light bulb and batteries, and special paint.

In general, Charlie is a disciplined and capable student. In my experience, it is rare for a student to have the self-knowledge and motivation to complete correspondence work* without benefit of class schedules and deadlines. Charlie has completed three such courses and is currently enrolled in a fourth.

Charlie is a creative and dedicated student who has accomplished a great deal and has a large capacity for future growth and accomplishment. I recommend him to you very enthusiastically.

In 2014, the Common Application School Report form included for the first time a School Profile section, but I also include a more detailed statement:

About Beach High School

Beach High School is one of several private schools offering high school enrollment in Santa Cruz County, California. I support students who, for two fundamental reasons, want to pursue their education outside of a traditional high school setting. Some students' interests, strengths, and talents are not well represented in the high school curriculum. These people go on to endeavors and vocations in the arts, business, sports, and practical crafts. Other students whose interests are more formally academic find little to challenge them at the high school level.

BHS graduates have been very successful at colleges and universities throughout the country, often very selective ones such as the University of California, Berkeley, the California Institute of Technology, Columbia, NYU, Reed, Rice, Stanford, Swarthmore, and many other schools. They have won numerous academic awards, and a substantial number enter graduate school.

I only occasionally provide individualized coursework; almost all credit is based on students' experiences elsewhere. The work for which I grant credit may include independent learning at home; work with mentors in the community; special programs sponsored by schools

---

*In the 1990s, distance learning courses were called correspondence courses, and lessons were completed on paper, mailed in, and comments and grades were returned by mail. Now such courses are mostly computer-based.

or other organizations; high school courses taken in public, private, and distance learning schools; community college and university coursework; volunteer work; travel; and training programs and employment.

BHS is in a suburban setting. Students are mostly White, with small minorities of Latino, Asian, and African-American young people. Because they frequently enter college early and thus have not completed sufficient coursework to be eligible for direct admission to four-year colleges and universities, about 80% of them begin at a community college and transfer later to a four-year school. Another 10% choose to nurture their talents outside of academia. The 10% who enter four-year schools directly have reached high levels of accomplishment through nontraditional means.

I have a California Lifetime Secondary Credential (technically a Life Diploma) and an M.A. in educational counseling. I worked for 32 years in public and private schools teaching in several subject areas and directing alternative programs in grades K-14. I taught at a local comprehensive public high school for the last 20 of these years. At this school I directed a program for gifted and talented students for 10 years (1980-1990), and my private school is essentially an expanded version of that program. BHS began operating on a full-time basis in 1993. Since then 1,456 students (as of September 2014) have graduated.

Wes Beach, Director

If you provide any kind of note and/or school profile or school description, it will undoubtedly be very different from mine because your homeschool is unique and has a very small number of people in it. I've included my note and school description not because of their content but for their tone and style, which I hope are very straightforward and surefooted in describing in some detail exactly what my school is and does. Whatever you furnish should have these characteristics.

Two Books

As you prepare for college (or while you're in college), you might find it useful to read the two books I describe here.

After interviewing a number of highly accomplished people and delving into research others had done, Ken Bain concludes in *What the Best College Students Do* that effective and meaningful learning—"deep learning"—is as much about personal development as it is about mastering subject matter. This personal development comes about when people take charge of their own educations and choose to learn in ways that are consistent with their personal values and goals. The "best college students" don't focus on earning high grades; sometimes they get them, and sometimes they don't. But they graduate from college and go on to live creative and productive lives. In my view, there's no reason why anyone needs to wait until or attend college to engage in deep learning.

At one point during a sendoff-to-college party my wife and I threw for the son of a friend, people offered advice to the young man. Mine was, "I hope you don't have to choose, but if you find that you do have to choose between getting good grades and learning stuff, choose learning stuff." I also said that I had learned a lot outside of my college classes. When I graduated I was very knowledgeable about John Steinbeck and his writing. I was a physical sciences/math major, and almost all of what I came to know about Steinbeck I learned on my own. I also spent a substantial amount of time outside of my education classes reading and thinking about schooling.

In *How We Learn*, Benedict Carey, a science writer for the *New York Times*, presents what science says about learning. Many guidelines for studying that have been promoted for a long time are not actually helpful, such as the suggestion that you have a regular place, maybe a desk, where you do all your studying. Carey explains that a complete understanding of how we learn doesn't exist, but he describes in an interesting way research that has been done and offers practical advice for effective learning. Here are a few of his recommendations. If you read the book you'll understand the basis for these and other suggestions.

- Study in different places, not at the same place all the time.

- Learn material in a series of several sessions, not in one long session.

- Don't simply read, say, a chapter in a textbook many times; read it a few times, close the book, and try to say aloud or write down what you remember; in other words, test yourself.

- Work on understanding several related ideas during a study session instead of focusing on one idea at time.

And remember, "I hope you don't have to choose, but if you find that you do have to choose between getting good grades and learning stuff, choose learning stuff."

Chapter 6
Two-Year Degrees, Other Programs, and On-the-Job Training

Becoming a Chef

Selene Johnson hated high school. She didn't feel that she fit in anywhere. She thought her teachers were just doing their jobs without caring much about students, and that they were often not very knowledgeable about their subjects. She began taking community college classes during the second semester of her sophomore year, and then took the California High School Proficiency Exam, passed it, and earned a Certificate of Proficiency, a high-school-diploma-equivalent certificate. This allowed her to leave high school behind.

After her short stay in high school, Selene spent four years taking classes at the community college. The pattern of courses she took made an associate's degree in Spanish the simplest to obtain. She completed the last Spanish class needed for her degree as a concurrently enrolled student at the University of California, Santa Cruz.

Her real interest, however, was not in school, but in restaurant work. During the time she was in college she was also working in restaurants, washing dishes, busing tables, serving as a hostess, cooking, and waiting tables. Her fellow workers provided a camaraderie that she had not found in college. She felt most comfortable working in kitchens where she and her co-workers formed a community of people who liked being up to their elbows in their work.

After earning her A.A., Selene moved to San Francisco, where she again worked in restaurants. She also worked in retail and at an architectural firm, where she gained computer skills and proficiency in handling paperwork and creating documents of various kinds. She wanted to attend culinary school, but couldn't afford it. She saved for a year and bought a one-way ticket to Europe, where she worked in kitchens for a little more than a year. Her desire to become a chef developed.

Selene returned to Santa Cruz and worked at various restaurant jobs, first focusing on pastries, and later working with caterers. Having acquired a wide array of skills, she set out on her own.

Fast forward to the present: Selene is now, because of her skill set, in demand as an executive chef. She not only has a deep knowledge of cooking, but also understands all aspects of food and event preparation, including budgeting, buying, staffing, and graphics. She says she spends about a third of her time on paperwork.

Selene's most recent job was at a modern art show in Miami that drew tens of thousands of people from around the world. Her responsibilities included establishing two popup outdoor restaurants, in one of which she oversaw everything necessary to serve sit-down meals to as many as 1,500 people. She also set up several indoor banquets, serving 5,000 people in some instances.

Although Selene has a college degree, it has never been essential in obtaining work, and her high degree of success is the result of on-the-job acquisition of an extensive set of skills. In telling me her story, she wrote, "The courage to initially leave the traditional route of schooling and to travel alone at a young age was encouraged by my mother who herself had the heart and curiosity of a wanderer. Since that time I have continued to travel and grow my skills. There is no school that can teach what is learned by being a student of the world, where I continue to 'study.'"

Many Resources for Education and Training, and Many Kinds of Occupations

Once while getting my eyes examined, I met a technician who took lots of pictures of my retinas with a specialized piece of equipment; the photos were then stored in a computer, sent to my doctor in another room, and stored in my file. This technician was quite willing to tell me the story of his education and his work. He had wanted to become a firefighter, so he earned a degree in fire technology at a community college. After completing his two-year degree, he wanted a job as an EMT, but he was unable to find a position he liked. But his education made him employable in the technician's position. He was sent by the doctors who hired him to a private institution where he learned phlebotomy so he could give injections, but he learned everything else, including how to use sophisticated equipment, on the job. He told me he had plans to learn more at home, using material provided by other private institutions, so that he could pass required tests and obtain a series of certificates issued by state agencies that would allow him to perform a broader array of medical procedures and possibly work at a hospital.

After my conversation with this technician, I discovered that there are many dozens of places approved by the California Department of Public Health where phlebotomy training is offered; these training programs are at adult schools; community colleges; private vocational institutions, schools, and academies; county occupational programs; hospitals; and medical schools. Not all of these places are colleges; training in phlebotomy (and in many other fields) can be found at a variety of places.

Don't assume that colleges are the only places where you can get the kind of education you want. I learned from a former student who is now a very successful wedding photographer that camera companies offer photography classes, and training in photography is also available at conferences.

There are many kinds of jobs that you've probably never heard of. Trying looking around in the Occupational Outlook Handbook at http://www.bls.gov/ooh/. As it says on the home page, "This is a guide to career information about hundreds of occupations!" You'll find job titles, job descriptions, the education needed for each job, and median pay.

In the next chapter you'll read the stories of other people who have created productive lives based on self-learning and on-the-job training.

Chapter 7
Succeeding Without College

Even if you're completely convinced that you want to go to college, consider not going. Doing so will make your decision more secure, whether or not you change your mind.

An excellent guide to thinking about college or not is Blake Boles' *Better Than College: How to Build a Successful Life Without a Four-Year Degree*. The book tells Blake's story and the stories of others who have directed their own learning, provides sensible and workable guidance for thinking about the direction of one's life, and includes advice from and reference to other sources. Most important, in my view, the book focuses on self-knowledge as the basis for a productive and fulfilling life, regardless of college.

Micah Harmon didn't think that college was his way into a productive and fulfilling life. He is a hands-on person. In high school, he struggled to sit still and focus and was easily distracted. During his senior year, he homeschooled, then applied for a BHS diploma. He had been working in a surf shop, selling surfboards and equipment, giving surfing lessons, and doing ding repair. A friend left a job with a pool company, recommended Micah, and he took the job. He liked doing this work outside, but he wanted more structure and better long-term prospects.

He did some research on the internet, looking for work that he would enjoy and that paid well. Micah decided on sheet metal work, signed up for the union's aptitude test, and did so well that he was placed high on a hiring list. Since he had signed up for both structural and service aspects of the test, he was interviewed, and as a result wound up even higher on the list. He was hired two months later by an HVAC (heating, ventilation, and air conditioning) company. He is now (August 2014) one year into an apprenticeship, with four years to go. He began learning his trade by making service calls with experienced people who served as his teachers. He arrived at my house on his own.

Micah now goes to biweekly eight-hour-long classes and has no trouble sitting through them to continue learning about the trade he's interested in. He realizes he is a smart person and wants to put to good use a brain that he knows works well. He wants to be a good service technician, challenge himself by learning to work on bigger jobs and more complex equipment, and possibly move on to become a service manager or a foreman. He knows he has a secure future in sheet metal and will be able to support the family he may soon have. In some instances, people who do HVAC work can earn six-figure incomes.

Making videos is a hobby of Micah's, and he may at some point challenge himself again to build his own video business.

Micah is succeeding without college, and I've worked with many others who have, without benefit of a college degree, found success in a variety of endeavors. Many of these people never completed four years of traditional high-school-level studies. They instead focused on developing their talents and reached high levels of accomplishment at young ages. Among people I've worked with or know are

- a principal dancer with a big-city ballet company

- a partner in a venture capital firm

- a singer, songwriter, and recording artist in New York City

- the co-owner of a restaurant (see Ciera Kash's story in *Forging Paths*)

- a leading man in the movies

- a well-known wedding photographer

- a circus performer

- a professional rock climber and gym owner

- a cosmetologist

- the owner of an auto body shop

And you've read about Smith Dobson in Chapter 1 and Chuck Heppner and Miriam in Chapter 2.

Finding Ways to Move Forward

The world presents you so many options for making your way, that I can't begin to tell you specifically how to get started. Still, keep the following in mind. Don't be afraid to contact people, even complete strangers, to find opportunities for yourself. My county holds an annual event, Open Studios, where artists open their studios to the public. Several years ago, I heard a glass blower talk of how he had learned his technique over many years, and how he had taught his young apprentice everything he knew in a year. Since then I have suggested to several people that, if they're interested in an apprenticeship in some art form, they could call the listed artists in the Open Studios catalog and inquire about becoming an apprentice. I've asked a few artists about this possibility, and they have all been willing to some degree. No matter what your area if interest—accounting, flying airplanes, working in politics, plumbing—use the phone book, the internet, personal contacts, random encounters, libraries, university catalogs, etc., to find people to talk with who work in the field interests you. Not everyone will have the time or the desire to spend time answering your questions, but many people will. I've had very good luck corresponding with authors whose books I've liked a lot. In two instances that I am aware of, former students found mentors (one in architecture, one in writing and illustrating children's books) by contacting authors of books.

Blake Boles' book *The Art of Self-Directed Learning* suggests many ways to make useful connections with people and explore the world. One of the book's chapters is titled "The Girl Who Sailed Around the World" and describes an adventure that in some ways was similar to Chuck Heppner's four years of worldwide traveling (described in Chapter 2).

Pursuing Dreams

Guy Thompson was my student in the 1980s, before I left the public school system to work on my own. Here's his story as he tells it.

My passion for the outdoors started at the age of ten when a man who was a friend of the family started a 4H group. He took us on hikes and taught us about our surroundings. I loved it. All that nature had to offer was intriguing, beautiful, quiet, and peaceful.

When I think about high school all these years later, I think that the teaching methods were a complete waste of time. One exception in my case was being able to choose my own elective classes. I took your Life Science class in 1988. I will never forget watching *Never Cry Wolf* the first few days of that class. The movie was an eye opener; I realized that I could actually do something like that if I desired. I had a passion for observing wildlife and the outdoors. After being the only kid in class who raised his hand when you asked, "Who of you think you'd like to do something like that?" you allowed me not to attend class but to read a life science book and check in once a week. Although our conversations were usually short, they had meaning. You would ask what I had learned and how it pertained to me. That helped because we retain what is important to us. Life is what we make it. My passions and dreams were my own, but I knew that I had to follow them. Things like finances and relationships got in the way of moving forward with those dreams; however, they were never far from thought.

I thought you might like to know that I am on my way to following those dreams. I now live in the wonderful state of Montana and even though I live in the capital (although small), I often find myself up in the mountains surrounded by wildlife.

After graduating from high school, I did what many typically do: nothing but enjoy the freedom of enjoying what's out there. Despite the hardships of life, I managed to keep myself from drugs or alcohol. I worked hard at various jobs trying to find what worked and discovered that starting my own business was where it was at. I used my creative side as well as personality to build a successful construction business doing everything from home remodels to commercial construction. I made a lot of money and enjoyed spending it on the people around me who were less fortunate. I'm not the type who has to have much of anything. A true believer of "less is more." Anyhow, when the economy dived, business died as well, and I found myself selling off equipment and tools to stay afloat. I came to the conclusion that California would never offer me the true happiness that I always dreamed of. With no obligation to California, I packed up and headed for the North Dakota oil fields to make just enough money to pay off the debt and make my move to Montana. Although working in the oil fields was probably one of the hardest things I've ever had to do, it worked. I first moved to the Flathead Valley (Kalispell/Flathead Lake) area, but again found it hard to get by with such low-paying jobs. So I moved again to Helena, Montana, and again had a hard start but eventually found a comfortable job. I drive a large truck shredding confidential documents. Believe it or not, the job pays quite well and I only work three-and-a-half days a week. The company I work for is based out of Spokane, Washington, and there are only three trucks in the state of Montana. I drive the central route from north to south. Again, I'm pretty sure that this isn't what I plan on doing for more than a couple years. As much as I enjoy the outdoors, I also enjoy cooking and baking. According to friends, I'm pretty good at it. Although I enjoy cooking and baking many types of food, I have perfected the "Burger." I managed to create burgers that I have yet to see on any food network and everybody raves about them. Hopefully in a year or two I'll be able to start my own "Burger Joint." The nice thing about this current job is that I get to meet some of the most influential people working for the state, county, and city. Some of those folks think that this town is in desperate need of a good burger. We'll see where time leads me.

I have learned over the years that giving back is also important. I became a counselor many years ago at a boys camp for SED [severely emotionally disturbed] kids. I was given the opportunity to start a cooking class that became very popular. Once in a while the kids would want to change a recipe so I would let them and then we would talk about why it's important to follow the recipe. I also explained that some ingredients can be changed but the properties of those ingredients needed to be researched first. I enjoyed watching the kids grow and, more importantly, two of my eight kids graduate.

As far as my personal life goes, I never married. I watched almost all my friends including my brother, get married and divorced, some more than once. I have waited and waited. I knew deep down inside that there was someone out there for me and believe I have finally found her. She is the female version of me. We act alike, we think alike, we finish each other's sentences and dream of the same things. It's absolutely amazing to be with someone that completes you. No fighting, no arguing, and believe it or not, only a few disagreements here and there. We are now engaged and looking forward to being together as one. I am the happiest that I have ever been. I wake every day thankful to be living in a place that makes me smile. Genie and I make a great team and I can't wait to see what the future brings next.

Surfing, Skating, and Success

Richard Novak became a surfer at a young age, and while he was in high school he spent many days surfing instead of attending classes. After he graduated he spent a semester at a community college, but, with a math instructor's input, he decided he could learn best outside of schools. He adopted a disciplined beach lifestyle; his passion was surfing.

Over the years Richard has gained the equivalent of a college education by learning from other people about subjects ranging from physics, chemistry, and composite materials, to accounting and business management. In his early twenties he talked his way into a position as a crew member on the research vessel Te Vega, operated by Stanford's Hopkins Marine Station. During the year that he retained this position he was able to sit in on classes aboard the boat, and, when on land, he had access to Stanford's library.

At age 19 Richard became a partner in Olson Surfboards, and his experience with this company "turned me on to the reality of business." In 1969 he and two partners started their own business that produced surfboards and sold all the supplies to make surfboards and boats.

He became a skater because he wanted something to do when the waves were puny. In 1973 he and his two partners formed NHS Inc., a company dedicated to selling skateboards. In 2013 it celebrated 40 years in business; it's the longest-enduring skateboard manufacturing company in the world. NHS Inc. employs about 95 people in Santa Cruz, California, and sells its products, including clothing, in more than 70 countries. NHS's website is at http://www.nhs-inc.com/, and you can read more about the company's history at http://www.santacruzsentinel.com/general-news/20131020/nhs-celebrates-40-years-of-skateboarding-innovation-and-the-creation-of-an-industry.

Succeeding on the Way to Earning a College Degree

Jerimi Walker (whose story is in my book *Forging Paths: Beyond Traditional Schooling*) earned a diploma from Beach High School; entered Troy State University in her home town, Dothan, Alabama; earned a degree; and went on to graduate studies at Syracuse University.

Her younger sister Cristl also earned a BHS diploma and enrolled at TSU, but then her diploma was judged to be not acceptable and she got the boot. She decided to follow her sister to New York, hoping that schools there would be more accepting. After a three-hour road trip from Dothan to Montgomery, she boarded a turboprop plane bound for Atlanta, her first flight ever. Once airborne she was enthralled, by being in the air and the wondrous machine that transported her. The longer flight to Syracuse, in a jet airliner, only intensified her fascination. Suddenly, she had a passion for planes and flight and a strong desire to become a pilot.

Cristl has crisscrossed the country, attending schools, holding down jobs, and undertaking entrepreneurial endeavors. After living in New York and attending a community college, she moved to Arizona, where she came very close to obtaining enough financial aid to attend Embry-Riddle Aeronautical University. She then discovered a much less expensive aviation operations program at St. Cloud University in Minnesota, where she then studied. Always needing to find ways to support herself, Cristl moved back to Alabama, returned to New York, and from there went to Denver, completing coursework at Metropolitan State University of Denver and, through distance learning, at Empire State College in New York.

Cristl found, in several locations, ways to connect with people in aviation. There were professors and pilots and others. There were opportunities to spend time in flight simulators. There was enough money to take some flying lessons. But the path to becoming a pilot was not yet clear.

Jerimi had become a math professor at a community college in a suburb of Chicago, and that city was Cristl's next destination. She found a job at a bank, and then at a brokerage firm. Becoming a financial advisor required passing tests and obtaining licenses, and it was necessary to obtain a sponsor to take the tests. Cristl's ability to gain the respect of her employers led to sponsorship, and she passed several tests, obtaining the licenses necessary to work as a client services representative for an independent broker-dealer in a suburb of Chicago.

Cristl now earns enough money to resume her flying lessons. Because of the time that has elapsed since her last lessons, she has to start over, but she regards this as an enrichment of her training. She will become a pilot, probably within the next four or five years. And a year of additional study will lead to a college degree, probably in applied math, a more widely useful degree than one in aviation operations.

Cristl's passion, confidence, and perseverance have been foundational in the pursuit of her dreams. When I asked her where these traits came from, she said she believes that they're a result more of nurture than of nature, and that the most important part of her nurture was being homeschooled, being able to structure her own learning rather than do what she was "supposed to do."

Whatever you decide to do with the next part of your life, . . .

. . . I believe deeply that it's your recognition of your genuine interests and talents and your self-knowledge, confidence, enthusiasm, determination, and sense of autonomy that will carry you where you want to go.

Chapter 8
Discarding Assumptions

In the passageways at a local mall there are seven-foot-high structures that display mall directories and advertisements. I was told by a person who works in the mall's management that these structures are called "monuments."

One monument has for quite some time displayed a large poster that depicts a young African-American woman working in a fast food restaurant. The lighting in this photographic poster is, I assume, purposely poor to add to its grim depiction of this young woman's situation, and her face does not stand out, but her expression can be seen. She's not smiling or looking happy, but it's otherwise difficult to discern her mood. She might simply be focused on what she's doing, or unhappy, or tired, or in some other state.

The wording on the poster is
Heather, 10th grade.
Worked 45 minutes on term paper.
Worked 9 hours on night shift.

I'm sure that the intention here is to create sympathy for Heather, relying on the cultural assumption in our society that young people should make schooling their priority, and that spending much more time at work than on school assignments is not a good thing.

These assumptions may not be warranted. But before considering this, there's the issue of inferring that the reported division of Heather's time is typical. It's possible that she has on other days spent a great deal of time on her term paper, and/or has set aside future times to work on it. Maybe she's a part-time employee and works just a few days a week. Perhaps she seldom works the night shift; it might even be that she's substituting for someone else and night shifts are never part of her own work schedule.

If the time division is typical, there are several possible reasons why Heather is giving her term paper short shrift. It may be that she is in distress because of her work/school schedule. But there are other possibilities. We don't know what class the term paper was assigned in, so let's assume the class is U.S. History. It could be that

- Heather simply isn't interested in history.

- her personality and the teacher's clash.

- writing is not one of her strengths.

- Heather is generally bored in school and prefers working.

- she is a hands-on person, enjoys being on her feet and active, and has a hard time sitting still at desks.

- Heather is hard-working and ambitious, and is destined to become the CEO of the company she is now working for. She knows that if she needs a college degree she can earn one without a strong high school record.

One of my former students worked in a fast food restaurant. I gave her credit on her transcript for doing so. She is now a doctor.

We all live in various societal and institutional cultures and experience pressure, often unnoticed, to absorb and adopt the beliefs and practices of these cultures. I taught in public schools for 31 years, left the system 21 years ago, and in many instances since then have had to work to consciously resist traditional assumptions. For example, for quite a while I felt that, when a student had spent some time in a traditional school, I was obligated to transcribe all of her coursework when I wrote a transcript. But I came to a point where I felt I needed to reconsider this, and decided I could list previously completed course work selectively as long as I made it clear on a transcript that I had done this. I've explained in Chapter 4 how selective transcription benefitted Anna Hutchinson.

There are many ubiquitous and false cultural messages about relatively small matters, like what a high school transcript has to represent, and about important issues such as how to begin a productive adult life. The central message is that if a young person doesn't jump through a series of hoops set in place by distant strangers, he will face a life in dead end, low-paying jobs and will not prosper. Homeschooling provides an opportunity to examine cultural assumptions, beliefs, and practices, including those of traditional schools, and, where state laws allow, to discard them and think creatively about how to create educational paths that allow young people to pursue their genuine interests and develop their talents. It could be that working in a fast food restaurant or at another low-paying job for a while would be the most useful thing for a young person to do. One of my former students spent part of her last homeschooling year working as an intern in a restaurant's kitchen. This internship was credited on her transcript, and it continued into the first part of a gap year, after which she went on to St. John's College, where she is now happily studying.

In *The Evolving Self,* Mihaly Csikszentmihalyi points out that our culture (along with all other cultures) represents a limited view of reality, and that its rules and habits are not absolute. The happiest people tend to live in many ways by their own rules.

Be happy.

Appendix
Resources

Your best resources are your determination, persistence, and creativity in finding the schools, programs, organizations, people, books, websites, and other supports that will be useful in your own self-directed learning. Here are a few books and websites that I have found informative and stimulating.

Books

Age of Opportunity: Lessons from the New Science of Adolescence, Laurence Steinberg (Eamon Dolan/Houghton Mifflin Harcourt 2014)

Better Than College: How to Build a Successful Life Without a Four-Year Degree, by Blake Boles (Tells Peak Press, 2012)

College Without High School: A Teenager's Guide to Skipping High School and Going to College, by Blake Boles (New Society Publishers, 2009)

Cool Colleges for the Hyper-Intelligent, Self-Directed, Late Blooming, and Just Plain Different, by Donald Asher (Ten Speed Press, 2007)

Doing School: How We Are Creating a Generation of Stressed-Out, Materialistic, and Miseducated Students, by Denise Clark Pope (Yale University Press, 2003)

Feel the Fear . . . and Do It Anyway, by Susan Jeffers (Ballantine Books, 2006)

Fiske Guide to Colleges, by Edward Fiske (Sourcebooks, updated annually)

Genius Denied: How to Stop Wasting Our Brightest Young Minds, by Jan Davidson, Bob Davidson, and Laura Vanderkam (Simon & Schuster, 2005)

How to Survive in Your Native Land, by James Herndon (Heinemann, 1997)

How We Learn: The Surprising Truth About When, Where, and Why It Happens, by Benedict Carey (Random House, 2014)

Making the Choice: When Typical School Doesn't Fit Your Atypical Child, by Corin Barsily Goodwin and Mika Gustavson, MFT (GHF Press, 2011)

Summerhill School: A New View of Childhood, by A.S. Neill (St. Martin's Griffin, 1995)

The Art of Self-Directed Learning: 23 Tips for Giving Yourself an Unconventional Education, by Blake Boles (Tells Peak Press, 2014)

The Childhood Roots of Adult Happiness: Five Steps to Help Kids Create and Sustain Lifelong Joy, by Edward M. Hallowell, M.D. (Ballantine Books, 2003)

The Evolving Self: A Psychology for the Third Millennium, by Mihaly Csikszentmihalyi (Harper Perennial, 1994)

The Talent Code: Greatness Isn't Born, It's Grown. Here's How., by Daniel Coyle (Bantam, 2009) (Note: I don't agree entirely with the premise of the title, but this is thought-provoking reading.)

The Teenage Brain: A Neuroscientist's Survival Guide to Raising Adolescents and Young Adults, by Frances E. Jensen, M.D. with Amy Ellis Nutt (Harper, 2015)

The Teenage Liberation Handbook: How to Quit School and Get a Real Life Education, by Grace Llewellyn (Lowry House Publishers, 1998)

What the Best College Students Do, by Ken Bain (Belknap Press, 2012)

Where You Go Is Not Who You'll Be: An Antidote to the College Admissions Mania, by Frank Bruni (Grand Central Publishing, 2015)

Websites

Blake Boles' Zero Tuition College
    http://www.ztcollege.com

College Confidential
    http://www.collegeconfidential.com/

Davidson Institute for Talent Development, especially the articles provided at:
    http://www.davidsongifted.org/db/browse_by_topic_articles.aspx

Gifted Homeschoolers Forum
    http://giftedhomeschoolers.org/

Homefires–The Journal of Homeschooling Online
    http://www.homefires.com/

Homeschooling A to Z
    http://homeschooling.gomilpitas.com/

Occupational Outlook Handbook
    http://www.bls.gov/ooh/

Peter Gray's blog, especially the piece at:
    http://www.psychologytoday.com/blog/freedom-learn/201108/is-real-educational-reform-possible-if-so-how

About the Author

Wes Beach worked in public schools for 31 years, mostly in high schools, and in a private school for one year. He taught science, math, and English, and directed programs for gifted and "at-risk" kids. He wised up in 1993, left the system, and has since then directed Beach High School, which consists of a home office and an attitude–the attitude expressed in this book. He is at present the Teen Adviser for both the Gifted Homeschoolers Forum (GHF) and the HomeSchool Association of California (HSC); he served on HSC's board for two years. He has spoken at many conferences (especially at HSC's each year), written a number of articles, and authored another GHF Press book, *Forging Paths: Beyond Traditional Schooling*. He is an outside consultant for the Davidson Institute for Talent Development, and in 2005 received a Distinguished Service Award from the California Association for the Gifted. For more articles by Wes, please check out the Articles page at www.giftedhomeschoolers.org.

Made in the USA
San Bernardino, CA
15 May 2020